COM·PEN·DI·UM

/kɒmˈpɛn.di.um/, [kɔmˈpɛn.di.ũ]

Essential Thoughts & Observations
for the Journey of Life

Pls. Review on Good Reads

TAL McABIAN

(818 402 9090

CONTENTS

TAL McABIAN

PRELUDE

Hello! My name is Tal (which means "morning dew" in Hebrew) McAbian. Though my name may elude to a different origin, I am a mixed Jew- Half Sephardic (Jews originating from Arab countries, North Africa or Spain) on my father's side and half Ashkenazi (Jews of Germanic and East & Central European descent) on my mother's.

Let me give you the backdrop- The period, place, sound, vision, smell and ambiance of the day and atmosphere of the time; from my arrival to the ensuing years of my early childhood.

I was born in London, England, during the spring of 1969 in a neighborhood known as Ealing; then mostly a Jewish community, now more Indian in nature. The world during the first decade of my life was an interesting place undergoing a tumultuous Renaissance (or "Re-Birth") brought about by numerous intersecting uprisings, warring philosophical views, differing lifestyle choices and ideological battles marked by the sexual revolution, the concept of the commune, practice of "free love", opposition to the Vietnam War, Ping Pong Diplomacy, the Watergate scandal and THE Scandal in the British Parliament, a society reeling from the wounds of the Watts Riots, the conception of Haight-Ashbury, the reign of the Hippies (an oxymoron, of course…), Woodstock Festival, tie-dye attire and psychedelic drugs.

Some fantastic cinema contributed as well. Some adaptations of the above and other gems, such as; "A Clockwork Orange", "Serpico", "French Connection", "Chinatown", "Yakuza", "Rocky Horror Picture Show", "The Godfather" trilogy, and of course the intimacy of "Love Story".

The VW Bug, Thing and Minibus were the vessels, Mr. Nice (not quite yet a book, but just a man), "Easy Rider", "Zen and the Art Motorcycle Maintenance", "I'm OK; You're OK", "Fear and Loathing in Las Vegas", "Chariots of the Gods" (proven a hoax apparently) and "Love Signs" (yet to be determined but, so far; so good…) as the narrative augmented by a dynamic and meandering soundtrack courtesy of some prolific singer-songwriters, including; The Beatles, The Doors, The Grateful Dead, Janis Joplin, Crosby, Stills, Nash & Young and Jimmy Hendrix (can you believe he would have been 75 this past November, 2017).

The musical Hair, the carefree days of the Flower Children, the time of Sgt Pepper & Yellow Submarines and The Age of Aquarius. Lava lamps, kaleidoscopes, political stickers, bell bottoms, afros, and thigh-high boots (which were meant to walk), robust student protests and social engagement such as the world has never witnessed before and they even put a man on the moon, whew!!!

It was nitty gritty, grassroots, Bohemian, revolutionary, swank and posh all at once- a kaleidoscope of movements and thought rolled into one reality. And then came me… What a time to be born. But… "*From chaos comes order*", so here we are.

I am no oracle, I do not purport to be a sage nor wise beyond my fellow man. I am however a sponge. I am observant, cognizant and aware, c'est tout. I read, watch and listen; always have, always will. I have been lucky enough to travel the world, visit many museums, learn about different cultures, examine their history, savor their foods and taste their women (yes, I just said that).

At what authority, under which auspices and due to what qualifications I have the right to write what I am scribing, you may ask…? None, really; at least not in a conventional way. I certainly did not graduate from Harvard or Oxford, do not have a PHD, other Doctorate, nor even a degree in philosophy, psychology, or political science. I do not belong to M.E.N.S.A., was never invited to the Bohemian Grove, spoke at a TED event, participated at the Davos Summit nor visited the Belfer Center.

I graduated from business school and learned the fundamentals of managing, branding and marketing different businesses. I have an affinity for history & political science as well as philosophy and psychology, but the latter subject matters are only an interest in my relentless pursuit for knowledge, nothing more.

I was also blessed and lucky enough to live a very rich life thanks to my parents and the traveling & exposure to other cultures and distant lands I visited- Requisites of my profession at the time.

I personally believe there are many sources of information and for learning and enriching our lives. Not only our parents, teachers and professors, but equally, doctors, politicians, lawyers, technology wizards, financial experts, titans of industry, music composers, authors, artists, script writers, actors, film directors, stand-up comedians, our parents; even our kids and pets (I'm dead serious..) and, of course, bartenders and barbers; sorry, hairdressers. All are mentors to me, as I believe they could be to you, and all contribute to our aggregate individual knowledge bank, our intellect and our understanding; of different disciplines, vocations, subject matters, fields of study and interest, of ourselves and of each other.

This knowledge and everything written herein is readily available- All I have attempted to do is harvest and present it to you in a succinct and comprehensible manner, adapted to the trials & tribulations presented in life today. This compendium of sorts includes the obvious (a lot of that, trust me), the forgotten or overlooked, and, hopefully, a few epiphanies will present themselves along our journey, perhaps some revelations will be unveiled and maybe you'll even come across an eye-opening fact, a useful analogy, a proverb you haven't heard before, a thought that rings true or a practice you'll adopt.

All that I have experienced to this very day- The people I meet, the lands I travel, and the music I hear, the food I savor, the scents I smell, the terrain l traverse and all that I see; all of it has been captured, harvested, classified, investigated and studied. Just like our digestive system, that which is beneficial, I keep; that which is not, I dispose of.

If you extract only the very best ideas, suggestions, information or whatever from every experience and rid yourself of the useless noise, jargon, traits, habits, people or things that only know how to demand, take or otherwise be a liability or burden and you will be on the road to realizing your maximum potential; in every facet of your life.

The objective of this book and that which I aspire it will instill is not changing your life; only you can do that. What I hope to achieve is enhance and improve your life in at least one aspect, maybe a few suggestions, ideas or habits you'll adopt, or your way of thinking in at least a single aspect of your life. That would exceed my grandest ambition.

It is now time to cleanse my palate, empty the vault and let every person who wishes extract as little or as much as he or she wants to.

1 THE BEGINNING

Whether by forced extraction or slippery descent, we are brought to life naked, devoid of any material belongings. When mortem strikes, we are returned to the earth just as nude, equally destitute- "*For dust you are and to dust you shall return*".

The period of time in between is that which I aspire to address and, hopefully, assist you with; the degree of facilitation that is endorsed and executed is entirely at your behest.

Writing this book is not my life's mission. My raison d'être are my children, immediate family, extended relatives and my close friends. In that order. Friends, unlike family, are chosen; you choose them and they choose you.

But we digress... My mission in life is my commitment and duty to those listed above. To shelter them, to share with them what I have learned, to ensure they are healthy; by educating them about preventative measures to quell ailment, taking care of them in time of need and responding to their cries of help. Do all that I can to ensure they have a sound mind and a healthy body in whatever capacity I can. Simply put, to help them enjoy a better quality of life.

I must also guide them, to whatever extent I can in deciphering their talent and area/s of expertise. At that point, I must assist them in honing, fostering and nourishing that talent so it is realized to its fullest potential and they, in turn, are satisfied, fulfilled, content and become the very best they can be in whatever path they choose to pursue. I am their protector, their catalyst and I provide the inertia needed to expedite and achieve this; given my capacity to do so of course.

If I (and you; to your own circle) do not do this and execute this task perfectly, all untapped potential and unrealized talent both go to waste. While that may not matter with most of our brethren, other than the specific individual in question and his/her immediate ecosystem of family and friends, think of the ramifications if the individual who could have conceived the cure for cancer is one of those lost souls.

This is the essence of evolution- The father teaches the child (or, the maestro educates and trains the apprentice) and, over time, from one generation to the next, with the technical advancements we make, our evolved minds and the seamlessness and ease in which we can share knowledge and information, this evolutionary progress is growing exponentially.

Life presents various challenges at different ages and under a variety of circumstances. People always say "wait until you graduate", or "wait until you start your career", or "wait until you get married", or "wait until you have kids", or "wait until your kids leave home", or "wait until you grow old" to illustrate how the pressure, stress, challenges and the obstacles will grow in severity and extremity. They may even cite some "what if's" or "if you only knew" (or "experienced", or "suffered", or "been through") to convey the same notion.

Yet, in reality, every age poses its own set of unique challenges and, while every person's life course, set of circumstances and narrative may differ, the stress level and pressure these challenges exert can be viewed as uniform at their arrival point.

Someone once told me, "leave one man and one woman alone on a deserted island. Return to visit them after a thousand years and you can be certain of two things: First, they have procreated and their offspring multiplied in numbers abundantly. Second, they will have established a religion and a code of conduct, a set of protocols for acceptable behavior and regulations to be implemented as their rule of law based on said religion."

While no theological expert, in my own journey of life thus far, I have come to notice that, at their epitome, devoid of the regalia and within their core beliefs, most religions aspire to teach the same dogma- benevolence, instill respect and compassion for others, teach virtue, piety and humility, dignity and integrity, encourage growth, chastity of mind, purity of soul, health of body, the courage to do what's right and simply to be an all-around better person. One who provides for his family, sacrifices for the benefit of others, contributes to his community, donates to society and enhances mankind.

They also aspire to foster harmony and a sense of balance, in every aspect of life. Some have even evolved to promote tolerance and understanding.

We are taught these principles through a strikingly similar set of laws, beliefs, practices and rituals because, apparently, the average human is too stupid to figure out he or she should not sleep with their brother's wife, kill their neighbor or disrespect their parents. Most of these will be explored in this book. As many of the topics and ideas transcend classification and cannot be relegated to one aspect of life, they will be presented in a fluid manner.

I don't believe there is some coveted repository of knowledge that is intellectually superior. I don't think

that the teachings of priests, muftis, rabbis, yogis,
nuns/monks (of all creeds) and other soothsayers &
sages, provided that are mentally stable and
emotionally healthy of course, differ all that much. In
this regard, there is no Holy Grail.

Further, beyond the commonality of beliefs and
teachings, it is interesting to point out the similarities
of rituals within the monotheistic religions. Some
examples are the concept of sacrifice, utilizing water
for purification, personal hygiene, behavioral codes,
family structure, the roles & responsibilities of the
different clan (don't worry, NOT that "Klan"…)
members, conduct pertaining to chastity, piety,
benevolence, et cetera…

Also worth noting is an observation related to the
Messiah of said religions. The Christians, et al, have
Jesus. The Muslims revere Muhammed. Yet us Jews
are still devoid of such a figure… Why? You may ask.
I suspect, as often is the case, because we are waiting
for a better deal…

The decisions we make pave the path we embark on
and the direction we pursue which ultimately dictates
our life. Religion, in it's purest form, should aspire to
give us the tools to make the right choices in life to
become that better person.

This book contains no new information or revelation. It merely documents, brings to light and promotes a discussion of the thoughts we all have, the challenges we all face and the choices we must all make. At best, it perhaps offers a different point of view to your own or a suggested course of action based on logical deduction and explained by reason. Some ideas will be eye-opening, while others well... not so much. Nonetheless, it is a journey worth taking and an expedition I'm sure you'll enjoy.

Since *"you can only bring the horse to the well, but you cannot make the horse drink"*, it is entirely up to you what to reap and what to put into practice.

Life is a gift- The most precious gift we will ever receive. It is therefore basic reason and logic that lead us to conclude we should do all we can to maximize and exploit it to it's fullest potential and to enjoy and experience all that we can.

Aspire to live, not merely survive or just go through the motions of life in a comatose state of ambivalence; as so many fellow humans do.

2 CHOICES, AMBITIONS, EFFICIENCY, COMMUNICATION AND PRIORITIZING

Strive to be the very best you can be in whatever you choose to do. With any luck, this will trickle, permeate, be adopted and practiced by your spouse or mate, children, friends, work colleagues and so forth... Imagine the aggregate effect and the cumulative benefit mankind would reap. But... *"Rome wasn't built in a day"*, so let's start with one person, you.

When faced with a dilemma, problem or challenge, we have to choose and the decision we make will inevitably carry repercussions, merit a response and have consequences. We must weigh the pros and cons, just as a balance sheet outlines finances, and decide a course of action and path to pursue. Barring intellectual capacity or mental stability, we should be able to choose properly. We should know right from wrong and be able to distinguish good from evil. That is not say we will choose the right option. At times, we knowingly choose poorly due to other desires, wishes or wants. At other times, we are manipulated by another's agenda or an ulterior motive.

My favorite film franchise is Francis Ford Coppola's cinematic masterpiece adaptation of Mario Puzo's novel, "The Godfather". Several years ago, I was lucky enough to discover Vince Gillian's epic television series, "Breaking Bad". More recently, I've had the pleasure of watching quite a few Netflix series chronicling the rise and fall of a host of drug lords; Pablo Escobar of Medellin, the Cali Cartel, Los Zetas' founders Arturo Guzman Decena & Osiel Cardenas Guillen and their infamous successor, El Chapo.

Other than a very sensual soundtrack, an occasional display of philanthropy and depictions of machismo, flagrant debauchery and sexual exploits that may appeal to a male of my pedigree in a moment of weakness, the common denominator of these men was that the choices they've knowingly made resulted in a very short life expectancy mired by fear, suspicion, mistrust, a constant state of paranoia, feelings of anxiety, delusions of persecution and pervasive conspiracies. Almost always living in hiding and constantly on the run. It is no way to live; not even to survive.

It is never a question of "if", rather, a question of "when", "where" or "who". After all, the more enemies one makes, the more vulnerable one becomes- not only from government officials and law enforcement, not only professional adversaries, not only sabotage from within by one's own aspiring apprentices and assassins, but also family members of every victim seeking vengeance; whether innocent bystanders, enemies or other casualties of war. Most likely, also the scorn of more than one woman; and, as we know all too well, *"hell hath no fury like a woman scorned"*. That is a tall order and a quite big capsule to swallow; every minute of every day.

"Only a thief thinks everybody steals". As such, these people can never enjoy a tranquil, peaceful existence. *"Tell the truth and you'll have nothing to remember"*.

As the opposite is the case here, there is no solace. The ominous pressure and the consistent level of stress manifest themselves by a burden much like that Atlas carried on his shoulders.

This of course is true for criminals of every type alike, not only drug lords; murderers, thieves, rapists, embezzlers, even cheaters or those who engage in adulterous behavior. In hindsight, which is of course 20/20, perhaps they would choose a different course.

Consider these four films spanning five decades- "Scarface", "Blow", "Wolf of Wall Street" and "American Made". All marked with stellar performances by true masters of "the craft", namely; Al Pacino, Johnny Depp, Leonardo di Caprio and

Tom Cruise respectively. All tell a different tale, yet the identical result prevails- crime does not pay.

Well, it actually does, but for a finite time frame and you'll never know when the end arrives, but, when it does, it'll inevitably be too late. As Sammy Davis Jr.'s "Baretta" theme warns, "*Don't do the crime if you can't do the time*". Of course you don't know who Baretta is- the protagonist of a crime drama television series by the same name from the 70's.

Upon closer scrutiny, it appears that even the conscious choice to be an upstanding citizen is self-serving and emanates from self interest. After all, who wants to live in constant fear, anxiety and paranoia with such a short life expectancy?

So, by pure logic, if self-preservation is an instinct you possess, the criminal world is not for you.

Humans generally have a strong will to live. Not just to live out their natural term, but to extend their living days as much as possible employing an array of differing methods; some yet to be proven, some logical and others which are more than questionable. In fact, of the five most common human fears, four actually are or are closely associated with death- death itself of course, fear of heights, of the dark and reptiles; only the fear of public speaking is not directly related to our mortality. For these reasons, a strong survival instinct alone should point people in the right direction. That said, humans do not make their life choices based strictly on logic, hence this clearly is not the case.

Most decisions present severe choices or a selection of actions to be taken. Just as conventional multiple choice test questions, one, perhaps even two, options are outlandish, extreme or otherwise not applicable nor viable. We are generally left with two alternatives to select from.

A slight, but related detour real quick: As an analogy to those one or two options you can immediately eliminate obstacles on the path of obtaining your goal; both in terms of human obstacles (or competition; whether within the same company or outside competitors in any given industry) and other easily extracted barriers or challenges

Back to decision-making. Intuition and the unconscious are powerful tools we may not be cognizant of all the time. For this reason, we are often told to go with our first choice or "gut feeling". Something in our sub-conscious is triggered and it sparks a memory, a feeling, even a smell that point us to a specific choice, unless you suffer from a bipolar or multiple personality disorder of course.

Without such a feeling, to ascertain it is correct beyond just "feeling" right and to independently validate a choice made, there are a number of tools and general practices we will explore that help point us in the right direction.

It is also worth noting that choices made devoid of the "Seven Deadly Sins", or "capital vices", which consist of pride, greed, lust, envy, gluttony, wrath and sloth (laziness/ apathy) which provide misdirection, the right choice is generally crystal clear.

Other related factors that may cloud our judgment and need to be considered, or accommodated for, are our own insecurities, paranoias/phobias, neurosis, biases and prejudices; and we should be honest, at least with ourselves, about these.

This leads to the age-old adage, *"don't judge a book by it's cover"*. Give everyone a fair chance to prove themselves and make everyone feel (and try to believe it yourself, because it is largely true, despite your own biases or prejudices) important, as an equal, appreciated, acknowledged and integral to your success; because they are... Needless to say, not everyone is capable of becoming a fighter jet pilot or appropriate to be a clandestine espionage operative, but it's worth remembering that those who feed these folks are also integral to their ultimate success.

That said, the more specialized and scarce a vocation is and the more difficult, lengthier (and usually more expensive a path to attaining that specific expertise, the more reverence that person garners and the higher compensation that specialty would normally yield.

It *"takes a village (to raise a child)"*, many soldiers to win a war, a lot of civil servants to run a city smoothly. In short, there are many moving and essential parts to any well-oiled machine, whether "machine" is being used as an analogy or in actuality. Each has a role to play, a task to perform, a job to do; and each is integral to the successful execution and triumphant outcome of any endeavor or initiative.

Speaking of this concept and the attitude of all those involved being a contributing factor and, back just over two and a half decades ago (Jesus, time flies) in my documentary-producing years, I was lucky enough (my dad put that epic deal together) to be part of the production and distribution of the first "encyclopedia-type" television series about China aka, the Celestial Empire entitled "The Cultural Cities of China."

Side note: It would have made more sense if the division of the episodes was topical or categorized by theme or subject matter (and would have immensely helped sales, if that was the case (not that I should complain…), but our Chinese counterparts wanted the series divided this way to highlight and increase interest (tourism, investment, etc.) in specific cities, hence we were relegated to their instructions). More about this business/product- related topic later. But we digress, yet again…

This was back in 1992, long before the country was as "open" or flourishing as it is today. In many places, I was the rarest of species- People looked at me as if I just landed from a galaxy far, far away. They examined me closely with their eyes. Some even caressed the hairs on my arms in sheer awe. I was a "*fish out of water*" and this was "Close Encounters of the Third Kind".

At any rate, as I was saying, in China, one of the most evident differences I noticed was that almost everything is elevated to an art form. Regardless of what they do or are responsible for, generally speaking, people take great pride in their work. Whether a noodle maker, a calligrapher, porcelain potter, silk weaver, Qi Gong instructor, or snuff bottle painter (yes, there is such a thing; quite exquisite too, check it out..), they all have two things in common: They all strive to be their very best at what they do and they all believe their work is essential for the greater good and for their people & country to excel & succeed.

As a result of my travels to China, I and my parents
have amassed a formidable collection of (ALL legal,
worry not) Chinese antiquities, relics and curios of all
kinds. Among them are some aforementioned snuff
bottles painted by the most respected artist in that
discipline, a black-only water color painting of a pack
of Kulun donkeys (one of thirteen donkey types
indigenous to China) from the maestro of that very
distinct art from. Yes, the artistry gets to that level of
detail.

That said, I am not a hopeless romantic, nostalgic
nationalist nor a communist sympathizer. I am a
realist. I take everything with a grain of salt, I examine
and investigate, then I come to my own objective, as
best as they can be (given my own, like everyone
else's, shortcomings noted herein) decision. As such,
the above is of course largely true to most traditional
endeavors and crafts and, just as importantly, a
product of an educational system, government,
military and media that have relentlessly instilled
nationalistic fervor in their citizenry's DNA.

Side note II: Since we're on the topic of China and
since this book does touch on commerce though a bit
further down, here would be a good place to interject
my thoughts about Communist, (or "Marxist" as it is
often referred to) or Socialist governments and their
economies.

In their purest form, BOTH Communism and Socialism are beautiful ideologies- An egalitarian society where everyone is regarded as equal and taken care of by the State: Birth, education- In early years, general studies; later, a specific vocation, universal healthcare, even a homestead, then of course social security for one's Golden Years. Everyone contributes to the motherland and, in turn, everyone is taken care of by the motherland. A very maternal, nationalistic, even romantic approach to governing. Alexandre Dumas, the French author expressed this sentiment with these timeless words; "*All for one and one for all!*". The strong and able take care of the young, the meek, the helpless and the elderly. Sounds romantic, even utopian.

The nationalistic fervor was accomplished in an ardent, often brutal, manner in the decades following Mao Tse Tung's Communist Revolution (of 1946-49) establishing the PRC ("People's Republic of China"), to a lesser extent in the three decades just prior, after the Chinese Revolution of 1911 which overthrew the Qing Dynasty and established the ROC ("Republic of China"), and in the millennia before under dynastic imperial rule.

Founded on the same principles and a similar dogma as that of Marxism, communes emerged in California during the anti-establishment movement of the 60's (though, truthfully, they appealed to people a lot more for the pot and the orgies). Similarly, in Israel, a significant amount of immigrants from Central & Eastern Europe who emigrated from Socialist countries, mostly alone without their families, established a network mostly agrarian-based economic cooperatives known as "Kibbutzim". Even today, Denmark has a similar set-up, but it is limited to communal co-habitation only.

Like most Communist and Socialist counties, these two forms of the same formula established in the Western industrialized world, have, over time, failed for the most part. Widespread abuse of power, rampant corruption, a high level of mistrust and gross class divisions were ingrained in these societies. Unfortunately, what Marxist philosophy failed to take into account was human nature. Interestingly, three of the "Seven Deadly Sins" (or... "Capital Sins" or "Cardinal Sins") were the obstacles to the success of this market philosophy- Greed, envy and sloth (the latter means reluctance to work/ laziness; don't feel bad, I had no idea what it meant either...). Simply put, these are an excessive form, or abuse, of one's natural faculties or passions. Far from being utopian, reality and these human traits sealed the fate of this dogma.

If you don't believe me, just watch the phenomenal 1980 indie film "The Gods Must Be Crazy". The film takes place in South Africa where the otherwise happy lives of an indigenous tribe are suddenly torn to pieces by one Coca Cola bottle which "falls down from the sky", i.e., "… the gods" (actually, a pilot in a propeller plane throws it out mid-flight) and introduces the tribesmen to the concepts of scarcity, ownership and feelings of jealously and envy; concepts and feelings they knew nothing about before. Following the calamities brought on by the strange foreign object and intent on restoring order and their blissful way of life, the tribal leader takes the bottle to the ends of the earth to throw it back to the god; and there begins our story.

One of the most important practices in life is to consider with immense scrutiny who we surround ourselves with and whom we befriend. Whether in our mates, personal circle, social acquaintances, business partners, work colleagues or professional associates. It is therefore critical to carefully assess and closely examine the people you surround yourself with and allow into your *"circle of trust"*, at it's different layers and it's various levels.

The first group of people I try to shy away from are those who, for whatever reason, are driven by ego. These people will make choices based on feeding their ego and vanity, rather than what is logical; and no amount of reason will prevail.

The others are folks who are deceitful. Whether they are people who wake up and think "who am I going to screw to earn my dollar today" or those who cannot be trusted to be loyal in any other way, you should steer clear as you'll never know, why, how or when they will betray you, but, rest assured, it will come. As it said, "*a crooked tree cannot be straightened*".

I try to completely eliminate any contact or a relationship with the two above-noted groups of people. Only if it is beyond my power and I must work or deal with them, I minimize any contact with them to the best of my ability.

The foundational elements in our lives are the people who form the very essence of who we are- Devoid of them, we will never achieve the vertex of our potential; with the wrong ones in place, we crumble into ruins. So, make sure to qualify who you let in and how deep you allow them to penetrate.

Here comes the first of (very) few (I promise) fables- That's how important I believe this life lesson is... Here goes: "A scorpion, being a very poor swimmer, asked a turtle to carry him on his back across a river. "Are you mad?" exclaimed the turtle. "You'll sting me while I'm swimming and I'll drown". "My dear turtle", laughed the scorpion, "if I were to sting you, you would drown and I would go down with you. Now where is the logic in that?"

"You're right!" cried the turtle; "hop on!". The scorpion climbed aboard and, halfway across the river, gave the turtle a mighty sting. As they both sank to the bottom, the turtle resignedly said: "Do you mind if I ask you something? You said there'd be no logic in your stinging me. Why did you do it?"

"It has nothing to do with logic", the drowning scorpion sadly replied. "It's just my nature". Simple, but oh so damn important.

So be VERY selective (even selfish in a sense) with who you call a "friend". First, we really don't need that many. Second, we must eliminate the "takers" (as… "*we are makers; not takers*") who just mooch and contribute nada. Third, if they don't provide you with any benefit (and I do mean "ANY"- Whether it be educational enrichment, a shoulder to cry on, a wet set of lips, tongue and a heartbeat at the end of your penis (and, OF COURSE, vice versa…your vagina), a workout buddy, hiking companion or partner in crime), then what's the purpose or benefit of the relationship anyhow…?

Given the above, it only makes sense for us to surround ourselves with like-minded peps who (hopefully) are "evolved and elevated", or "high vibrational frequency" individuals. Gravitate towards those advanced beings and you are more likely to practice a healthy & fulfilling lifestyle, thus more apt to attain success, love, harmony, solace and happiness.

Like all else, it's really quite basic and simple- Be surrounded by happy people; you're more likely to be happy. Engulf yourself with intelligent and interesting folks, you might become one too one day.

At my wedding, the marriage officiant who wed us in Red Rock Canyon told me he used to be a cop in Long Beach, California. In his previous vocation, he encountered degenerate thugs, filthy drunks, nasty criminals from all walks of life and pretty bad energy overall. Nowadays, as a presiding official for marriage ceremonies, everyone he comes in contact with is happy, clean and positive; not to mention the tips...

The notion of practicing selectiveness, censoring the content when needed and being very mindful of what you divulge to whom also extends to ANY and ALL dissemination of information. It is said, when someone asks your name, answer "Nikola"; only when they ask your last name, do you say "Tesla", capiche...?. So, unless you are coerced or drugged, please try your very best to avoid verbal diarrhea.

The ability to control the flow of information is essential for success because, simple put, "*Information IS power*". Tell people only what they absolutely need to know at any given time; i.e. spit it out strictly on a "...need to know basis". As William Shakespeare wrote in "Henry IV": *"Discretion is the better part of valor"*.

The topic of information is extensively researched and discussed in Cesar Hidalgo's book "WHY INFORMATION GROWS- The Evolution of Order, From Atoms to Economics"; very much a worthwhile read.

Proximity to others matters as well. Those closest to us can do the most damage. As an example, imagine some stranger yelling "asshole" at you from across the street. Now, imagine your mother calling you an asshole. One you'll not remember a minute later; the other, you'll never forget. As such, barring family, tread carefully before letting your walled garden down and your sanctum to be breached. That "sanctum" being your circle of trust of course.

Conversely, you should be succinct with your words, the thoughts you convey and feelings you express. These will differ greatly depending on the audience of that which you are conveying.

As much as possible, whether it pertains to directions, a set of instructions, an email, letter or other information, employ the concept of *"K.I.S.S." (Keep It*

Simple Stupid); also conveyed a bit more eloquently by Albert Einstein when he said: *"Everything should be made as simple as possible, but not simpler"*. Well said indeed!

Also worth noting, whether good OR bad, if there is no sincerity behind your words, don't waste them.

You always need to measure the amount of information, level of confidentiality, degree of complexity and the scope of the language used so it, just like your demeanor, fit the intended recipient/s. This is a function of age, intelligence, physical condition, mental state, attention span, interest and, most importantly, where does the recipient fit within your circle. In which layer of proximity and at what level of trust.

Of paramount importance in today's world is to always keep in mind that, with very little initial information about another, one can damage you beyond repair, so don't make it any easier. For the record, when I say "damage" I don't mean identity theft, which is so commonplace, but still just simply a crime.

What I am referring to is defamation and slander on social media and/or by the planting of false information. Even a small "seed" can propagate, be manipulated and snowball within minutes. This can destroy your reputation and tarnish your image beyond repair; also within minutes. Beyond these sinister schemes, there's of course cyberbullying, cyberstalking, cat fishing, exclusion, impersonation, outing, trickery, denigration, flaming, disinformation, misinformation, shaming and the occasional troll to watch out for. By the way, if you are unfamiliar with any of these terms, I highly suggest you become acquainted with them as these are the weapons of the day.

As such, you MUST, and I cannot stress this enough, evaluate, examine and constantly scrutinize your online "persona" (or reputation) in terms of unfavorable and/or untrue information, posts or other communication which can adversely affect your good name and standing. Needless to say, this needs to be accomplished with your company, the products or services it provides and anything else that "lives" online in some form and can be damaged or tarnished. By the way, this gave rise to a whole industry managing people's online reputations and good standing.

And FORTIFY- Just as you fortify your home and your office with blinds, lights, alarms and security cameras, do precisely the same for your online presence, or "digital persona".

On the other hand, it is also integral and an essential sign of maturity to be able to look in the mirror, admit what's off, a liability or where you are at fault (at the very least to yourself) and remedy these detractions to the extent warranted and to the best of your ability. Don't believe you own PR, don't get high on your own supply and don't drink your own nectar. In the same line of thinking, *"just because you've been bumped up to first chair in the orchestra, does not mean you can compose a symphony"*. Anyway you phrase it- Be honest with (at the very least) yourself about yourself.

Which brings me to a related suggestion, of sorts… Try to find the silver lining in everything. Most, if not all, of the things we go through in life do teach us a positive life lesson, present an opportunity that did not exist previously, or present a solution we never thought of to a pestering problem.

To the extent possible, stay composed and focused, even under adverse conditions- Just like the very annoying, very trite and very over-used English proverb- *"Keep calm and carry on"* or the adage: *"That which does not kill you, only makes you stronger"*. Nelson Mandela perhaps said it best with these words, *"It always seems impossible until it's done"*.

Being honest with yourself does not just mean "manning up" to your bad deeds or "owning" your mistakes and trying to rectify & remedy both, it also means admitting your strengths and weaknesses and making sure you cover your shortcomings with other colleagues or co-workers.

For example, I am technologically inept. As a result, I do my best to surround myself with talent that will fill that specific void for me or on my behalf. Not one person is proficient and knowledgeable in everything and, if you strive for true perfection, you must combine forces; this alliance drives one another and pushes you, as a collective force, farther than you would ever reach independently. In essence, *"The sum of the parts is greater than the whole"*.

Just look at some of the greatest achievements and evolutionary milestones of mankind- From the dawn of the industrial revolution to the "Traitorous Eight" who ignited the digital revolution and the seeds it sowed, from Linux to Microsoft, Apple, Wikipedia and so much more...

Side note: More on the "Traitorous Eight" as well as the birth of both Venture Capitalism and Silicon Valley & the evolution of high-tech can be relished (yes, it's THAT good) in Dan Geller & Dayna Goldfine's epic documentary special, "Something Ventured" (available on Netflix, or, as I call it, "Harvard for the 21st Century").

Speaking of your fine self, just as noted above with regards to those whom I said I have a duty and obligation for, it is of paramount importance for you to investigate and identify your own talent or skill so you too can hone, foster and nourish that gift to it's fullest potential.

Albert Einstein once noted, *"If you ask a fish to climb a tree, and it'll spend it's entire life believing it is stupid"*. Everyone has a disposition and a talent for a specific pursuit and, if we all do strive to maximize our lives; both for our own benefit and that of our surroundings, that endeavor is the one that should be followed. True wisdom is knowing one's designated lane- his or her's sense of purpose. Some are scientists, while others are artists, but both are needed for us to evolve. Some are destined to lead, others make perfect soldiers, but both are needed for us to win.

"Do what you love and you will never have to work a day in your life…", a proverb expressed in many ways and attributed to multiple sources dating back to Confucius, but so true. Again, adopting this will be advantageous not only for you, but also for the benefactors of your work, as it will undoubtedly will be stellar. It will also extend to your circle of family and friends as you'll inevitably be content and fulfilled, a pleasure to be around, harmonized, balanced and ready to contribute to whomever may need a hand, opinion or other help.

Is it not racist to say that, generally speaking, Cuban, Caribbean, Brazilian and African kids have a better rhythm and can manifest an audible beat to physical movement in a superior manner to North European or North European kids. Quite simply, it is genetics. The genetics which evolved due to Darwinism. It is Darwinism because the first group of children live in a warmer climate, hence spend a considerable amount of time outdoors more than the second group so they can dance better. Simple.

One of the greatest books I have ever come across (and actually read...) is Professor Jared Mason Diamond's epic "Guns, Germs and Steel". Mr. Diamond is a professor of geography at UCLA. He is also a biologist, ecologist, anthropologist and best-selling author; quite the Vitruvian Man.

Curious, inquisitive and intelligent, he has contributed much to human understanding and evolution not only to those he taught, but with several seminal literary gems. Beyond the aforementioned work of genius, he wrote "The Third Chimpanzee", "Collapse" and "The World Until Yesterday".

In the course of his quest for knowledge, Mr. Diamond travelled to Papua New Guinea extensively for research purposes for about five decades. In one of his visits, a native Papuan named Yali posed the following question to him: "Why do you white men have so much "cargo" (a term in the local language which denotes material goods); and we New Guineans have so little...?".

Mr. Diamond also wondered why such a large percentage, about two thirds, of the world's 6,000 languages were present in Papuan dialects and how come such a significant portion of the world's caché of flora & fauna, around 80%, were present in the islands. The answer to these queries culminated in the Pulitzer Prize-Winning book "Guns, Germs and Steel", first published in 1998.

One of my dreams was to adapt his literary masterpiece into a documentary series. It was going to be one of my two "Swan Songs" from the world of documentary production and factual content about two decades ago (the second was a series about the danger of the inevitable forthcoming water shortage, how we have plundered this precious resource and ways to replenish it's supply), but National Geographic beat me to it, alas...

Two other books worth noting (and your time) are "Sapiens: A Brief History of Humankind" and "Homo Deus: A Brief History of Tomorrow" written by Yuval Noah Harari, a professor in the Department of History at the Hebrew University of Jerusalem.

So, look at the mirror, examine yourself (AND be honest with thy self, otherwise, this is an exercise in futility), then decide what you will. Radioman from the video game "Spec Ops: The Line" (yes, I've resorted to quoting video games... though, in all fairness, this adage did originate somewhere in the bible) said..."*The truth is hard to hear, but it needs to be said*"- This is true amongst real friends towards one another. Recognize who you are and take responsibility for your words and your actions. It is a cardinal rule for success.

Further, accept who you are and, remember, it is OK to have vices (no one is perfect; and that's a gross understatement), so long as you're aware & curb them. Even Abraham Lincoln said: "*... folks who have no vices, have very few virtues*".

And PLEASE do not, under any means, escape reality or the truth by practicing what the ostrich does to hide- Stick their head in the ground (with the rest of their body exposed), thinking if they don't see anyone; no one can see them.

That said, once you do make a decision or choose a path, pursue it with relentless vigor, absolute resolution, unbridled commitment, a sense of purpose and a clear goal in mind. Don't do anything half-assed. If you do all that you can and do it with conviction, obviously you'll be increasing your probability for success. In every endeavor; and in any walk of life.

Henry Ford captured this belief and notion unequivocally by saying: *"Whether you think you can or you can't, either way you are right"*.

As stated above, one of my life's foundational mantras, as trite as it may sound, is *"... Give everything you do 110% and you'll elevate the ordinary to the extraordinary"* (this one's mine). This holds true for absolutely EVERYTHING we do in life- From folding laundry, to cooking a meal, writing a report or sales presentation, planning a date, having sex and everything in between. This, by the way, is precisely why Pixar has never made a losing film, not even remotely close to one in fact.

Insofar as this practice unfolds in our lives; the above manifests itself as, *"...Some moments are worth remembering; others are unforgettable."*

This is why I believe that, *"if you want something done right, do it yourself"* (not the most prolific statement, I admit). This is largely because only YOU know what "right" is for what you envisioned and hoped to create.

Needless to say, we cannot "invent" extra time, hence, if you feel your day is full, prioritizing what needs or deserves improvement (and those things which would best benefit you and your goal) are those you should strive to be more attentive to and give that extra 10%.

Which brings us to a related concept- Opportunity cost. All scarce resources, natural or manmade, that are of any value (except for hugs & kisses) are finite. Thus, if you have $100 and spend them on "A", you cannot spend them on "B". The same notion holds true for time, energy, attention span and so on...

As such, ALWAYS be cognizant and aware of what you are missing, giving up or forfeiting by prioritizing "A" over "B"; and ALWAYS make sure that order is correct and true to that which you want.

Given the above, there are several similar derivative notions to consider in our behavior, as follows:

First, as the bestseller by Richard Carlson is titled, simply put, "Don't Sweat the Small Stuff...". The book goes further than that, but that's where I stop. Expressed as "don't be a "drama queen (or king)", "don't make mountains out of molehills" and a thousand other ways.

So, don't instigate, cause commotion, unnecessary drama, etc. for no reason. Of course it is the opposite if doing so suits your course of action and helps attain your goal and/or desired outcome, but more about that scenario later.

Second, pick your battles. Again, as resources are finite, choose those battles that are worthy and worthwhile to fight. When my stepson asked if he can get a tattoo (mind you, this was fifteen years ago, not in today's completely "inked" society), I just gave him a blank look. Following further probing regarding my approval and pestering me with the merits of defacing his flesh, I simply said: "You're a teenager, I limit whatever energy I have for fighting with you cover three topics- Education, drugs and sex." In my eyes, all else is frivolous and not worthy of engagement.

Third, focus those same resources on whatever moves the needle and gets you closer to your goal. To the extent needed for evaluations, comparisons or other analysis related to your modus operandi, do not waste time gossiping, making assumptions, conclusions or talking about how or why people got to where they are, whether they deserve it, yada, yada, yada... FOCUS on yourself and expend your time, energy, etc. on attaining your goal.

Fourth, don't waste time, energy or other resources on that which you cannot change (or help, or save, or whatever…). As Reinhold Niebuhr wisely noted: *"God grant me serenity to accept the things I cannot change, courage to change the things I can; and wisdom to know the difference"*. Absolute genius.

Next is of course how to maximize these resources. For starters, as briefly mentioned already, time- A most precious and absolutely finite asset.

"Carpe Diem" (*"Seize the day"*), a Latin aphorism from Horace's work, Odes, dating back to 23 BC, the 18th century writer and statesman, Johann Wolfgang von Goethe's proverb, *"Nothing is more important than this day"* and the much more recent John Lennon adage, *"Life is what happens when you're making other plans"*, all allude to the same notion- Make every day count and live every day to it's fullest.

Benjamin Franklin expressed this sentiment a bit more eloquently when he said: *"Dost thou love life? Then do not squander time for that's the stuff life is made of"* augmented by: *"Lost time is never found again"*.

"Mann tracht, un Gott lacht"; an old Yiddish axiom meaning *"Man plans, and God laughs"*, or, as James Dean noted: *"Dream as if you'll live forever. Live as if you'll die today"*. You never know when the cloaked grim

reaper wielding his scythe will pay you a visit. Four out of five people die, really... As for me, I intend to live forever- So far, so good.

"Now trumps the future anytime- The future is a sucker's bet; a maybe, a contingency, a what-if..." (James Spader's scintillating "Raymond Reddington" character; "The Blacklist" television series). But we digress yet another time...

This notion is perhaps best captured by the timeless children's classics of "Winnie the Pooh" authored by Alan Alexander Milne and expressed in the following words:

"Yesterday is history, tomorrow is a mystery, but today is a gift. That's why we call it the present".

Beautifully said Winnie! And, if you want to learn more about both the overt and subliminal philosophical messages which appear in these precious children's books, check out "The Tao of Pooh" by Benjamin Hoff.

So savor every moment- Every experience, every visual, every sound, every taste, every scent and every touch.

And mark every milestone- Celebrate every victory, every anniversary, every holiday, every birthday and every memory.

Expand this beyond just your own milestones. Thanks to social media and digital schedules, it is now easier than ever to mark your calendar and be alerted on birthdays, anniversaries and other special occasions for those whom you consider dear. A congratulatory phone call, a personal text, Tweet or post in the appropriate online community, perhaps a small gift that you won't even have to leave your chair to select, order and have shipped to the celebratory party. Small gestures that go a long way and make people feel exceptionally

After all, "*if we don't mark the milestones, we're just passing with the time*" (Malin Åkerman's "Lara Axelrod" character; "Billions" television series).

That said, life is not a sprint; it most certainly is a marathon. As such, a long-term vision and planning ahead, just like a chess match, are warranted and much preferred to a knee-jerk reaction as we are often tempted to succumb to.

To optimize our efficiency, we need to accomplish a number of things. First step- Do whatever we can to create an environment that will foster placing us in "the zone" and enable us to maximize our productivity. This is why certain companies offer a flexible work schedules, different work spaces, the option to work from home at times, have employee cafeterias, a daycare center, even foosball or massages, depending on their philosophy, corporate habitat and, of course, pockets.

As for you, evaluate your immediate work environment- Consider the lighting, temperature and music or ambient sound present. Examine the layout of your work desk, consider the comfort of your seat, the clothes you wear, does the file cabinet closest to you hold the folders you need most and so forth. Very basic, very simple, yet so often overlooked or entirely ignored.

Naturally, this extends to the comfort of your attire, your hygiene, your mental state and emotional condition. As such, try as much as possible, to make sure the "basic needs", at the very least, are quelled and appeased.

In broader terms, join institutions, embrace practices and create environments that cultivate and foster productive thinking and effective execution.

Parents who are successful and aspire their children to be the same, or surpass them, not only hope, but also pave the path for their kids to get admitted into an Ivy League school. It is not only for the education; it is equally for the social circles they will become part of and the networking they will be enabled to participate in.

It is no coincidence that most productive and successful people adhere to a very disciplined regimen, adopt strict rules of how they, and those around them, should conduct themselves, and are, generally speaking, pretty severe in response when even the slightest faux pas takes place; regardless if by themselves or others. These folks are often described as sufferers of OCD, at times even neurotic and practitioners of many rituals (the latter largely rationalized by these practices becoming second nature, thus accomplished by "auto-pilot", thereby, by their logic, saving time as well as conserving brain capacity to explore and divest in more interesting and, hopefully, more fruitful tasks & endeavors). Remember Ben Affleck in "The Accountant"…?

To an extent, this is also true for all maestros of creativity- The best chefs, composers, cinematographers, musicians, designers of all disciplines, programmers and researchers, among others. In general, they are very detail-oriented, extreme perfectionists, meticulous in their work and usually follow a strict code of conduct. For lack of a better term, they "institutionalize" themselves within an ecosystem they build, even within themselves.

The line between genius and madness is very faint indeed...

And, lastly, with regards to all the environments you operate in- Make them ergonomically comfortable, placate your senses as best as possible; basically, adapt, modify, design and stage these areas for maximum efficiency and productivity.

In essence, do all you can to be like a Marine at all times- *"Ready, willing and able!"* (and *"Semper Fi"*; *"always faithful"*, but that trait is covered elsewhere...).

Keeping all of that in mind, we know that life is far from perfect and will present obstacles, pitfalls and challenges we must persevere and overcome. To that end, it is important to learn the difference between "optimal" and "maximal". The former, "optimal", refers to perfect conditions, or as best as we could have ever hoped for. The latter, "maximal" denotes an imperfect reality; i.e., true or actual conditions. In both cases, how we operate and navigate varies greatly of course.

Don't deny your basic needs. Primal needs are essential for our survival and it is obligatory they are quelled. As such, try, as much as possible, to cater and attend to them as quickly and as often as you can.

You should always be hydrated, well fed, well slept and, well... well fucked. So, drink when you're thirsty, eat when you're hungry, sleep when you're tired and have sex when you're horny. As often and much as needed.

Just promise me you'll do your best not to deny these existential requirements. It is the first of many steps on the journey to success.

That said, you should of course control yourself in order to comply with the law of the land, the rules and regulations of the society you are a member of (or visiting) and, hopefully, step up and behave in accordance with moral norms and ethical conduct. Hopefully, this all makes sense and comes naturally to you. If that is the case, congratulations! You are a decent human being. Simple.

This ability to control our impulses- From having a filter that censors our words and adapts the way we speak and what we say (I personally don't have one, but I've heard they're absolutely splendid!), to restraining ourselves from raping the first mammal that struts in front of us each time we have an erection, is a VERY good thing and the one that separates us from our counterparts in the animal kingdom.

Side note- In case you are wondering, with regards to AI ("Artificial Intelligence"), the two things that separate homo sapiens (that would be us), would be consciousness and creativity, but I assume those differences will be bridged soon as well...

A full 20+ years ago, back in the spring of 1997, IBM's computer Deep Blue beat world chess champion, Garry Kasparov. At the same time, AI techniques were too elementary to beat a professional Go player and only reached the amateur 5-dan level. Go is considered more complicated than chess for AI, because its much larger branching factor make it prohibitively difficult to use traditional AI learning methods, such as; alpha-beta pruning, tree traversal and heuristic search.

That said, and saving you the milestones along the way achieved by several AI programs developed along the way- Zen in 2012, Crazy Horse in 2013. In 2014, AlphaGo was formed by Alphabet's DeepMind lab in London and started teaching AI by the utilizing deep learning.

To make a long story short, on October 19, 2017, AlphaGo Zero was unveiled- A version without human data and stronger than any previous human-champion-defeating version. By playing against itself, AlphaGo Zero reached the level of AlphaGo Master in just over three weeks.

At the end of May, 2017, the evolved AlphaGo Master beat the world's top ranked Go, Mr. Ke Jie, a monumental achievement for AI's progress. Since that time, AlphaGo was retired and the DeepBlue team that worked on it has been disbanded and is now focused on research in other AI areas.

Second side note- "(Technological) Singularity", the instance in which the invention of "Artificial Superintelligence" will abruptly trigger a renegade technological "growth spurt" resulting in unfathomable changes to human civilization. Under this theory, an upgradable intelligent agent (such as a computer running software-based artificial general intelligence) would enter a "runaway reaction" of self-improvement cycles, with each new and more intelligent generation evolving more rapidly than it's predecessor, ultimately causing an "intelligence explosion" and resulting in a powerful superintelligence entity that would, qualitatively, far surpass all human intelligence. A fugitive compendium of knowledge, if you will... And you will bow down to your computers and robots, someday... When, you ask...?

Some say that "Singularity" will happen only a decade from now, in 2028. The median estimate is actually 2040, but don't smile quite yet...

In 2016, Facebook's FAIR ("Facebook Artificial Intelligence Research") elected to terminate an AI experiment involving two chatbot "dialog agents" which were trained to negotiate using machine learning. The chatbots were good pupils and negotiated blissfully, but researchers soon realized the bots were creating their own language, diverting from human languages.

In essence, the model that allowed the chatbots to converse freely, using machine language to incrementally improve their conversational negotiation strategies as they communicated, eventually creating and using their own non-human language.

Not quite singularity, but this unique and very significant spontaneous development of a non-human language was probably the most shocking and thrilling of the research, but it wasn't the only one. The chatbots learned to be smart and manipulative about negotiating to improve their outcome. For instance, they pretended to be interested in something that had no value to it in order to "sacrifice" it later as part of a compromise. Not fully understanding what was going on, the researchers opted to terminate the experiment post haste… You know damn well this is NOT the end of this little Pandora's Box…

In the same field, on May, 2017, researchers at Google Brain announced the creation of AutoML- "Auto Machine Learning"- An AI capable of creating its own AI. By the fall of 2017, this advanced AI created an "offspring" (VERY disturbingly referred to a "child"), that outperformed all of it's human-made counterparts. Good luck everyone!!!

We all know what could happen when our very basic, or innate, human needs mentioned a bit earlier are not met. When we don't have enough water for our kids, sufficient food for the sustenance of our family, when we are deprived of a proper night's sleep, or when a sexual appetite is not placated. The consequences of depravation are all bad. The only variance is the degree in extremity of the forthcoming calamities- A momentary lapse of reason (great record too, BTW; Pink Floyd, in the event you missed that..), temporary misjudgement, agitation, anxiety, anger, despair, embezzlement, theft, fury, rage, violence, assault, burglary, robbery, a fight, a battle, a war, molestation, incest, rape and whatever other heinous catastrophes I may have neglected to list.

On a much lighter note, a tale recounting how completely consumed Albert Einstein was by his

thoughts and theories and how absolutely immersed
he was in his experiments that he would often not
only forget to eat (as do many writers, architects,
researchers, painters and others when "in the zone"),
but that his lab assistant would often call his home
sometime after he left his office at Princeton
University to ascertain Mr. Einstein did make it home
as he would often lose his way when in deep thought
akin to a state of trance. Further proof to the old
adage that "...*Not all those who wander are lost*...".

Our work space mentioned above touches on the
concept of Feng Shui, a system of laws considered to
govern spatial arrangement and orientation in relation
to the flow of energy, and whose favorable or
negative effects are taken into account when selecting
a site to develop and in designing structures or spaces.
Like many other disciplines and philosophies, Feng
Shui withstood the test of time; and that which does,
carries at least some merit. As an example, it calls for
a bouquet of flowers or wall art to hang at the end of
a long hallway so people have a destination to look
forward to when walking down a corridor. Simply
put, it is why certain establishments feel inviting and
welcome and some do not.

The teachings of Feng Shui apply not only to your
office space and home, but that philosophy can be
extended to your car, gym and any domain you create
or find yourself in. So, organize and design, for both
ergonomic comfort and for maximizing efficiency and

productivity, your absolute perfect environment- For your thoughts, your words, your schedule, your work area, your relaxing corner, your sleeping quarters, your car and your life. Some of these we've covered; others we will soon.

It is also important to do your utmost and accommodate your own natural peak productivity hours- Are you a morning person or a night owl...? Artists, researchers, writers and composers generally prefer to work at night- The darkness, the solitude, the quietness; that's when their mind is clear, information flows, thoughts are formed and they are at their best. Others need the commotion, social setting and endless stimuli of an office and the sun's biological clock-setting qualities of daylight hours.

Likewise, some people need a sense of urgency, or deadline, to perform at their best; others need time and peace & quiet to operate optimally.

Making your time count, being as productive and as efficient as you can be involves a careful (and true) understanding of the concept of "Opportunity Cost"- doing one thing is always at the cost (or opportunity) of doing another. This includes monetary consideration, time, energy, work, or any other tangible object or scarce resource; just as theorized in the Newton's third law of physics.

"There is no free lunch- Everyone has to pay; grass, gas or ass…". There inevitably is ALWAYS a cost for the execution of a task or job and the attainment of a product or service. If it's time lost, energy exerted, money paid or any number of other resources expended, the laws of physics always apply.

Now that the value of time and understanding of opportunity cost have been evaluated and explained, the task of prioritizing needs to be addressed.

Prioritizing requires that you assign value to the different variables making up the algorithm that should, in a perfect world, dictate your schedule. The values you assign are derivatives of conflicting agendas within your world in every aspect and at every level; both macro and micro.

For instance, proper prioritizing is not only a consideration between work and family, but also between son and daughter within the confines of the family. Like all else in life, here too a true and concise consideration can get very detailed, down to the minutia. Just like fractals in nature, so are prioritizing (then scheduling) in life.

So scheduling should inevitably result in what (you consider) most important, most pertinent and most beneficial taking into account time sensitivities, difficulties in accomplishment and possibilities of delegation of at least some or one facet of the scheduled task or event.

The above applies for all analytical prioritizing/scheduling- an agenda for a board meeting, your daily or weekly "to do" lists, and, yes, even life's good ole' "bucket list".

There is a natural order of things or tasks to accomplish, things to get done and for events to unfold. In a perfect world, these all have logic and reason dictate their ranking in terms of importance, relevance and urgency. That order is unique to each of us and a function of numerous factors, such as; what we individually consider of higher importance, of more relevance and more urgent to complete or accomplish.

Needless to say, this order is gravely disrupted when we are distraught emotionally, pressed for time or otherwise pressured to get somewhere or accomplish a certain task, regardless if the source of that undue stress is our boss, a client, a work colleague our parents, siblings, children or a combination thereof.

Procrastination on another's behalf or someone else's urgent matter does not constitute an emergency on your behalf. Well, they should not, but they unfortunately often do.

In Judaism, it is believed that anyone who reads the "Zohar" (literally meaning "Radiance", it is a collection of commentaries on the "Torah" (Old Testament) which form the foundation of the "Kabbalah" (Jewish mystical teachings), too early or when not "ripe" enough to do so, both in age and appropriate theological level, might lose their sanity and become emotionally unstable.

The point is, just as when you know you're not quite able to perform a certain physical feat (regardless if you are too young or over-the-hill), smart enough to play chess against an advanced player, or a ripe enough lawyer to take on a complex case, you should equally be able to decipher, prioritize, then schedule yourself and your life according to the same logic; i.e., according to your capabilities at the time.

Similarly, preparation, preventative measures and being ready for whatever life, or work, present along the way are tantamount to success. It's ALWAYS better to be safe than sorry.

In the film/television production business, like in construction and almost all other "project-driven" industries, a day of pre-production (i.e., BEFORE filming commences, hence a much cheaper expenditure) can save production (or post-production) days; both of which are substantially more expensive. As in fiction, so in reality...

The same doctrine applies to our personal life- For example, how you rear your children and try to guide them in the right direction, how you regard your health and everything in between; "... *An ounce of prevention is worth a pound of cure*"- Clever words by a wise man; Benjamin Franklin.

All relationships, in their bare and most basic form, are quite simple to assess. A relationship is either good or bad for you. It either benefits or damages you, brings you up or down- Simple. But, alas, life isn't that simple- It is complex, poses many challenges and presents a host of variables, many outside of our control and all which must come into consideration. And many relationships unfortunately exist due to one of these three (very) unfortunate circumstances- Financial dependency, sexual dependency and, quite sadly, yet very simply; habit...

True love, as my ex mother-in-law, said so perfectly, is loving someone NOT "because of...", rather, "despite of..." and the feeling, to me at least, which describes the ultimate relationship is perfectly captured in the following words: "*Good things are hard to come by in this life, and you've given me more than my share*".

To those who you truly love and respect, give the greatest gift of all- That of absolute truth. In both words and in action.

As in all other healthy interpersonal relationships, the foundation of all work-related ones is based on three major ingredients- Trust, respect and communication. While the first two need to be earned and, under perfect conditions, should be reciprocal and equal, communication is the one we can influence most.

Communicating clearly and succinctly is imperative. Convey your message, the information you wish to or assign the tasks you are delegating in the most explicit manner possible to alleviate ambiguity. This of course varies and a function of both the information being transferred and the intended recipient.

It is believed that up 70% of communication is non-verbal (studies actually vary in terms of the actual percentage, but the figure is significant). Non-verbal communication is the transferring of information by non-verbal means, i.e. body language. There are four common ways to communicate- Face-to-face, over the phone, handwriting, and, lastly, by typing/ texting.

Face-to-face conversation is best as it engages more than one than one sense and thus provides more information than other types of communicating- In this case, we do not simply hear the words spoken, but can also listen to the sometimes very subtle intonation and inflection of the voice (to decipher mood, intent, even importance or sense of urgency) and can watch the body language (largely for the same reasons).

The second most information laden form of communication is speaking over the phone. While the visuals are gone, the words themselves are there, as is the articulation of the voice.

Third is handwriting- Again, the words are there, at least visually, and so are some hints as to the mood & intent of the scriber and the importance of his/her words.

Finally, the least amount of information it transferred with typing/texting. Here, all we have are naked words, devoid of ornaments and regalia. Words carry different meanings to different people, they write differently, their vocabulary varies greatly, even cultural differences (not to mention generational ones...) affect both the message and it's interpretation. Beyond this, in today's world, people expect an immediate response and any delay may cause baseless assumptions and unfounded conclusions to be made.

Whether it's capitalization, the grammar, missing an acronym here or there (after all, in what other form of communicating, you need to clarify you are joking by noting an "LOL" or "JK" to avoid any misunderstanding), not to mention today's overall lax attitude towards spelling- Everything has it's nuance and contributes to the subtle changes in desired meaning and decoded interpretation. This is apart from the, heaven forbid, occasional delay in response- Regardless whether the reason is you are choking, trying to avoid a car accident or a result of being in the middle of a board meeting or if you don't reply where you were two hours ago, God bless you soul...

Just examine the above four types of communication, reflect at your own misunderstandings with others and rank the probability each holds for a potential misunderstanding, disagreement or fight. Chances are, the less information is transferred (hence, the more left for assumption or interpretation); the higher the probability of discord.

Bottom line, try to select a means of communication, whether it be informative or directive, that best conveys your intended message in a succinct manner, with clarity and devoid of ambiguity.

Considering today's different platforms for communication and human interaction (and the relevant considerations of time management, prioritizing and scheduling), as well the virtually endless ways we can exchange information available today by typing- The role they play in our lives (how prevalent they've become so that some, such as; "texting", "messaging", "posting", and "Tweeting", have become actual verbs in our spoken tongue), and the time they cost us, so yes, opportunity cost applies here too.

So ponder these platforms, if you will- email, text, MMS, Instant Messaging (under it's variety of brand names); Facebook, Instagram, Snap Chat, Musically, Tumblr and Pinterest posting; What's App, We Chat, Line, Yaari and Baidu; those that seem like ancient history now- MySpace, hi5, Plaxo and Friendster; professional networks, such as LinkedIn and countless other industry-specific virtual communities and social networks; others whose common denominator might be an interest, a hobby, a sexual or mating preference...? or Meet Up, where you can just create your own community and, finally, we cannot overlook the myriad dating/fucking/hook-up/mating sites.

So many ways to communicate with one another! And so few have been reduced in kind- just a handful the digital ones and, in the realm of reality, only telex and faxing (though the latter is still used from time to time).

An onion of many layers, it is reminiscent to the different planets and galaxies in sci-fi film franchises or the levels of thought embedding and mind manipulation in the film "Inception", or even the Russian Babushka doll-within-a-doll. Just as with these examples, our means of communicating are just a tad too plentiful. They consume so damn much of our precious time and you most certainly have and will forget to comment or reply to someone; or "like" something; or post or share with others, inevitably upsetting or alienating quite a few people as a result. A   true   labyrinth   of   chaos.

3 PROFESSIONAL PROTOCOL, COMPANY CONCERNS AND WORK-RELATED PRACTICES

Now, let's *"get down to brass tacks"* (if you ever wondered, as I have, there are two theories as to the origin of this saying- One dating back to 1863 Texas in reference to enable precise drapery measurement, the second, from the same period, makes reference to the practice of using brass tacks to spell out the name of the deceased on the coffin. Here, some more useless information, but, as with all information, it will come to use; sometime, somewhere…).

As cliché as some of these may sound (and, admittedly, they are), it never hurts to see them written out and remind yourself of these practices and habits:

As a business owner, make sure to have a clear, concise and understandable Mission Statement as well as a clear conceptualization of both goals and the desired path for obtaining said goals. Make sure you have good, talented and loyal people. Evaluate each and identify their area/s of expertise, specialized talent/s and specific strength/s so that they operate in a capacity enabling them to maximize their contribution and benefit and enabling them to shine.

As an employee, make sure you fit the company's "ecosystem" and that its culture is one you'll be able to thrive, grow and be your very best in. Likewise, make sure what you're about to embark on is of interest to you so that you maximize your probable longevity, thus your potential advancement and compensation.

As either of the above (owner or employee), you should evaluate the intra-company dynamics and politics within your organization, then optimize or mitigate each; wherever and whichever way that is possible.

As mentioned above, materialize your thoughts by writing them down. Before, we discussed this as a safeguard so that you won't forget your great ideas, but equally as important, is to transform these intangible ideas into something tangible (or at least represented in a physical form); in essence, bringing an idea from the realm of imagination and hope to that of the reality. Just as those goal boards work.

Maximize that which you control- Your effort, determination, motivation, the quality of your work and the time you put in to perfect it. Fear is natural-

Whether it is the fear of failure, the fear that something will not succeed or fear of competition, treat fear as a motivator, not a handicap. Those that have no fear are a danger, many times even a lethal detriment.

And work- Work as long as it takes and as long as needed, but never to the point of committing "Karōshi" (the Japanese term attributed to the very disturbing phenomenon of death by overworking).

Numerous considerations need to come under constant scrutiny and certain factors under continuous evaluation in any company; regardless if you are it's founder or one seeking entry-level employment in it. These include assessing every member's performance, productivity/ output and process. Appraising their adaptability to the work environment and fit to the company's culture. Their contribution in terms of original ideas and fresh suggestions in the realm of R & D, new product/s improvements, new product/s, new product lines; their marketing initiative ideas, or promotional campaigns designs. Their biases and prejudices. Their desires, goals and modus operandi for attaining these; and if that MO is in line the enterprise it is to serve.

Study and assess the competitive landscape in an honest and realistic manner, see where you fall and whether it makes sense to pursue the endeavor you are involved with. It is paramount to objectively

evaluate if your product or service is feasible and
viable.

As indicated above (and repeated here verbatim as
this concept is THAT important...), once you have a
clear goal and chosen MO ("Modus Operandi", or
"course of action"). Sorry for repeating from the
beginning, but this is immensely important, so here it
is yet again... Once you do make a decision or choose
a path, pursue it with relentless vigor, absolute
resolution, unbridled commitment a sense of purpose
and a clear goal in mind.

This sentiment was illustrated succinctly and captured
by Winston Churchill with the following words:
"Winners never quit, quitters never win".

Again, do not do this to such a level where reason has
been replaced by futile idealism and/or vanity. That
said, if you do firmly believe you are correct and on
the right path; AND, if logic sides with you, "carry on
my wayward son...". There are numerous staples in
our lives, whether in consumer goods, entertainment,
art or culture, that almost didn't see the light of day
or, conversely, were not a hit or runaway success
when first introduced or launched.

Steve Jobs was ousted by the board of Apple Inc., the
very company he co-founded with Steve Wozniak in

1977, only eight years later, at which point he acquired 50.1% of Pixar (becoming the largest shareholder in Disney when the latter bought Pixar in 2006) and founded NeXT, only to return to Apple 11 years later and introduce the first iMac in 1998; two short years after his triumphant return, but 21 very long years after he co-founded the company.

Microsoft's Bill Gates and Paul Allen initial searches for funding did not prove to be a smooth patch of road either, initially rejected by anyone they approached for investment.

The trials and tribulations of Francis Ford Coppola and George Lucas, two of Hollywood's most prolific producer/directors, with American Zoetrope up to the making of The Godfather (to be followed a couple of years later by Lucas' own epic franchise, Star Wars among countless other seminal films) were very bumpy and debt-ridden, namely to… Warner Brothers.

To put this in context, despite their hardships and setbacks over time, at the time of scribing this book, these two companies are the world's top valued corporations by their market capitalization.

Equally, the examples cited below from the entertainment industry also persevered and overcame tumultuous paths to eventually become the apex of film & television.

Gene Roddenberry's science fantasy "Star Trek" franchise, as popular as it has been for the past five (yes, five- it made its debut in 1966 on NBC) decades was in fact cancelled after only three seasons.

While M.A.S.H., the 1970 feature film by Robert Altman based on a novel by Richard Hooker, won the Palme d'Or in the Cannes Film Festival and five academy awards, it's sequel was created after an attempt to film the original book's sequel and it too had a hard start- After all, who wanted to watch a satirical black comedy about the Korean War when the wounds were still fresh and we were in the midst of the Vietnam War...?

On the subject of timing, it too is paramount in any endeavor- When an idea is made public, a company is launched, a marketing campaign initiated or a new product is released. Timing is indeed everything.

An example of great timing, most definitely not in any way to detract or take anything away from Vince Gillian's absolute genius (nor the masterful portrayal of Walter White by Bryan Cranston), but I suspect at least a minor factor to his outstanding "Breaking Bad" television series' success was its timing. The series made its debut on January 20, 2008; just months before the economic collapse of August, 2008, which almost lead to the complete demise of the world economy and most dire recession (by most measures, actually a depression) since The Great Depression of 1929.

Contrary to many television series' viewing history, "Breaking Bad's" popularity only grew with time culminating in a spectacular trajectory towards the show's finale, a Bell Curve pattern followed only by other monumental series at pinnacle of televised entertainment.

I for one can attest that, like many others (it appears), identified and found semblance in Walter White. The concurrent emergence of the two events noted above most certainly didn't hurt ratings... And, as time passed, so did the show's popularity; precisely how events in the global economy unfolded and we realized just how very fucked we all were... And could identify with Walter's justification of why a man who suffers from a terminal lung cancer while earning $43K/ year as a high-school chemistry teacher (far from the millions made by his much less intelligent former partners at Gray Matter Technologies which he co-founded as a promising chemist) can rationalize his slow morbid descent into purgatory and the moral detours needed to become the monster he ultimately transformed into; a man known as Heisenberg, an homage by Mr. Gillian.

Side note: For posterity's sake, some of the other television series which followed a similar Bell Curve, include ("but are not limited to"); "I Love Lucy" (1957), "All in the Family" (1979), "Taxi" (1982) "M.A.S.H." (1983) "The Jeffersons" (1985), "Cheers" (1993), "Seinfeld" (1998) and "Friends" (2004).

Back to timing. I myself faced the fate of ill-timing during one of our nation's most despondent times, just after 9/11… Yes, I had a televised direct marketing campaign for a multimedia kit called "BODY SIGNALS- The Power of Body Language". It was a body language tutorial consisting of a DVD, book and style-chart for dressing.

This self-improvement program was created by two of the foremost experts in human behavior and development, Dr. Jo-Ellan Dimitrius, a best-selling author and jury consultant who came to notoriety during the O.J. Simpson murder trial and Patrick Collard, a corporate strategist, body language and elite security expert.

It was the perfect personal development system that taught people how to read body language so they can decipher the hidden (and real) truth behind their words as well as improve their own body language, thus enabling them to convey their intent and message clearly and concisely. In short, it would provide whoever studied the kit with an edge and the knowledge to empower both their personal and professional relationships; and it even preceded "The Mentalist" and "Monk" by years...

But the world just wouldn't have it. Understandably, everyone's attention was focused elsewhere and the perfect product turned out to be a bust. Too bad for me.

While we're on the topic of conveying the right message, it is imperative to always anticipate what is expected and play the part. What I mean is that you dress appropriately for the occasion at hand. If it's a job interview, dress in a manner fitting the corporate culture of the entity you are visiting. If it's a black tie affair; guess what, wear a black tie. If it's a Western-themed company BBQ, wear your plaid flannel shirt, bolo tie, your chaps and cowboy boots adorned with spurs. So anticipate AND perform the part; whether it's a board meeting, sales presentation, marketing pitch or an interview. Simple.

The same of course applies to your behavior, demeanor, language and so forth. If there kids around, no cussing. If you're in court, be courteous and respectful. Also simple.

Ever notice how every retail establishment you walk into is perfectly curated...? The overall design, decor style, color palate, how products are displayed for sale, how new releases are showcased and highlighted, the room's temperature, the lighting and, of course, the background music. Just like you, EVERYWHERE you shop is tailor-made to appeal and cater to the designated client's tastes & preferences. The more they feel welcome and at home, the more comfortable they become and the more they spend. Yet again... simple.

On a related note, a friend of mine owned several supermarkets. Their design is such so that you would have to traverse the whole store to find only a few items. The more you walk, the more you run into stuff, the more you run into stuff, the more likely you are to buy items other than those you specifically came in for; inevitably leading to a bigger sale.

Just like the joke about Costco, the gargantuan U.S.-based mass merchant, goes: "A man walks into Costco to buy his wife tampons. He walks out with the tampons he came for and a boat. When asked why that is by a curious bystander, he replies: "Well, my weekend was shot anyway, so I figured I'd go fishing". Not necessarily a true story, but you get the point- When did you ever walk out of Costco with ONLY what you originally intended to buy...?

What you name a company, product or service, for multiple reasons, is also of paramount importance. Obviously, an easy to remember, catchy name that represents what the company, product or service is, a name that is fitting for your target audience and market segment and is in line with the company or brand's mission and image they wish to portray. You should also consider S.E.O. ("Search Engine Optimization") when naming anything and, if applicable, what that name means in other countries, cultures or languages. Yes, all of these are important and integral for a successful venture.

What's in a name you ask...? Years ago, at a time when I was still producing and selling films, I had drinks at the Carlton Hotel during the Cannes Film Festival with a colleague who was an international salesperson for Warner Brothers. He told me "Tal, I have one of the greatest films ever made to sell this festival, but it'll be a flop theatrically at home (the U.S.)". "Why?" I asked puzzled and bewildered. "Because of it's name" was the reply.

The movie, by all measures, is a phenomenal cinematic work of art. It is considered one of the greatest films of all time in every notable such list. And it did, relative to it's enduring popularity, the awards it garnered and consistent high ranking, perform terribly in terms of domestic theatrical revenues. It's initial theatrical run generated about 30% less than the film's budget, let alone it's P&A ("Prints and Advertising") expenditure. At that point, the combined loss (production budget and P&A, minus box office receipts) was about $25 million; and the year was 1994. Luckily, once word got out and over many years of broadcast airings, over time the film more than made it's money back and much, much more.

The motion picture was "The Shawshank Redemption". Based on the Stephen King novella "Rita Hayworth and Shawshank Redemption", it was written and directed by Frank Darabont and showcases Morgan Freeman (who was not portraying God for once) and Tim Robbins at their very best.

Side note: Kudos and much respect to the amazing Stephen Edwin King (aka his pen names, Richard Bachman and John Swithen) for this and so many other incredible literary works, mostly in the horror, supernatural fiction, suspense, science fiction and fantasy genres. His body of work consists of an astounding 200+ short stories (one of which was this particular film's origin), 54 novels, and is responsible for some of the greatest literary work adopted for film, including; "It", "The Shining", "Carrie", "Creepshow" and the timeless "Stand by Me".

Regarding international business, although the world is getting "smaller" and the cultural divide is almost completely gone these days, it is still worth knowing the customs, rituals and practices of those you encounter or interact with. Bringing a gift when first meeting with a Japanese client, if and how deep to bow, the notion of apologizing when the encounter commences and so forth. In devout Muslim countries, the role of women will inevitably differ from any Western industrialized country, as will the "if, when and where" with regards to the consumption of alcohol and the emphasis on hospitality; most specifically, dining.

These traditions, customs and nuances dictate the protocol of how a meeting (and business overall) should be conducted; from the initial greeting to signing a deal. Where it pertains, there are specific practices and norms of behavior concerning gender, job position/rank or age differences between the two parties as well as how socializing in general and alcohol consumption specifically are regarded among business associates.

Try to find the "hook", or differentiating factor (maybe several), that your product or service possesses or offers and highlight this benefit as much and as often as possible. There has to be one (preferably, more of course) unique characteristic that sets the product or service you're peddling apart and differentiate it from others.

So, take that "hook" (better yet "hooks") and your "story" (of that of the company, idea, product or service; whatever you are currently soliciting) and make some noise people!

This means PR ("Public Relations"), press releases, news and updates, whatever; just make sure there's always something being told and talked about- An idea, your thoughts, a new product, a completed installation, a successful solution, a new project, a satisfied customer, a future plan or goal; really... Whatever.

Originating as a soda fountain beverage in Vicksburg, Mississippi in 1886, Coca Cola's sales were impressive, but not stellar. Eight years later, it was sold in a common glass bottle called a Hutchinson and sales grew substantially. Yet, only when the Root Glass Company of Terre Haute, Indiana, won the approval for their unique contour design in 1915, one of the few packages ever granted trademark status by U.S. Patent Office, did Coke sales skyrocket to the sales level and market penetration the drink enjoys until this very day.

The proprietary hourglass bottle ultimately became the "hook" for Coca Cola- It distinguished the product, made it unique (with the aid of the patent, forever...) and crowned it a runaway hit that never looked back. The brand awareness of Coca Cola and devout customer loyalty it enjoys remain unrivaled by any single product until this very day, over one hundred years later. Quite simply, it is the greatest brand that ever was.

Sorry for the diversion, now back to getting the word, any word, out. The subject matter needs to be fresh, insightful, beneficial or positive to those whom you are attempting to entice, your target audience and prospective clientele. It needs to be delivered in a clear and concise manner which is conducive to you the message you wish to convey, information you want to share or directions you want to give (i.e., print (if so what font, size, color, etc.), imagery or other visual medium (whether still or video/film clip and, again, what "style", "look and feel", how sound/music interface with the visuals, etc.).

Basically, the most fitting campaign that suits the company's culture, fits its image, represents the product or service and evokes the desired emotions (and, hopefully, actions) from the customers you wish to attract or market segment you are targeting while respecting and, when and where possible, strengthening the brand's identity.

Sounds complicated? It sometimes is, but sometimes it's not- It's just a matter of hitting the nail on the head. Example? One of the longest-running identical physical coupon campaign I remember is the "Bed, Bath & Beyond" 20% off any single item one.

With its blue border, it always looks the same. The large dark blue text on the white background is simple to read. The offer, as noted, is identical- 20% off any single item (and it never expires…). The paper stock is not too thin so easily tears, but not too thick so it is difficult to fold. It is oversized so it stands out, but not too large so it poses any inconvenience and keeps falling or folding over from your car door's side pocket or wherever you store it. And, since it's always honored, people usually do not discard these coupons and generally have them within arm's reach, thus making "eye contact" with you and always keeping the retailer fresh in your mind.

I believe that there are many factors which led Bed, Bath & Beyond to completely command this retail sector (at least in the western U.S.), but am certain this genius, seemingly never-ending, coupon offer is a major, if not the dominant, reason for their dominance in this market.

As Albert Einstein brilliantly stated: *"Everything should be made as simple as possible, but not simpler"*.

The dissemination of this information also varies greatly; not only from one industry to another, but over time- From physical brochures to digital websites; from conventions to online forums, even You Tube channels; from industry paper magazines or periodicals to industry-specific social networking communities; from industry-specific associations to virtual communities and commercial online platforms.

The key is of course to identify the best and most effective "information vessel" of the day, utilize it to the best of your knowledge employing whatever "tools" there are to ensure the most efficient and saturated penetration possible as well as metric analysis programs available at the time to assist in evaluating your performance, execution and standing and to maximize your exposure and benefit.

Marketing, promotion and public relations are disciplines unto themselves. We are just covering, from a very macro-perspective, the general principles, topics and notions related to getting the word out-About you, your idea, your company, your project, your service, whatever...

Perhaps my favorite PR/marketing-related triumph is the charade that one company, almost single-handedly, fed this planet for over a century- De Beers and the inflated/ perceived value of diamonds.

Diamonds were made desirable by a brilliant century-long marketing campaign coupled with an almost absolute monopoly of the supply of these stones, at one point controlling 90% of the world's diamond supply, which enabled this South African company to regulate almost all the stones that made their way into the world's jewelry shops.

As seemingly scarce and almost sacred diamonds have become in our society, in nature they are in fact quite unremarkable. While they do need a fair amount of pressure to form, they are simply crystals of carbon; and carbon is the fourth most abundant element in the universe. As such, they are believed to be the commonest gem-stones on earth. Elsewhere in the cosmos, as was recently established by a paper just published in Nature Astronomy in late 2017, they are probably available in embarrassing quantities. Yet, somehow, we were convinced otherwise; of the exact opposite in fact. Coupling that with our herd mentality as a species, spent vast amounts of money to acquire them and hold them with such reverence and high regard until this very day.

Our "herd" mentality is of paramount importance in the marketing, promotional or PR campaigns of any product, product line, company, idea or even elections. Just as a bad review by a professional; or a few from consumers (even fake ones…), can kill a product. Just as a Tweet by the right entertainment or sports celebrity or the right actor endorsing a perfume or cosmetic product; either his/her own line or simply as a spokesperson (because actors know so much about either…) can make a product a resounding success.

This mentality transcends consumerism. In Hebrew there's a well known passage in the story of Passover. Just before Moses split the Red Sea (sure...) and the Jews found a safe passage, albeit rushed, from Egypt to the Sinai Peninsula en route to "The Promised Land", they lamented about *"who knows who the next Pharaoh will be..."*. Meaning, as bad as this one is; enslaving us, torturing us, shackling us; both physically and emotionally as his slaves, at least it's an evil we know, are familiar with and, despite the hardships, manage to live with. The same exact logic is used when battered spouses rationalize the actions of their abusive mates, or those living with addicts; of all shades, say to excuse their behaviors...

Being such creatures of habit means us humans are inherently resistant and afraid of change (the great "unknown"), even if all the evidence points to a brighter future. I recall learning about a study that took place in a large office space divided by those lovely gray-toned, half-height cubicles. A productivity expert came and decided the recessed lighting needed to be dimmed a bit. What happened to productivity, you may ask...? It increased substantially. A few days later, the expert returned and decided to do the opposite- Make the recessed lighting considerably brighter, much more so than the original luminescence in fact. What happened to productivity, you may ask yet again...? It increased yet again by a notable margin.

So, how is that possible is the only question left, right...? Upon surveying the employees, most indicated they didn't know what this expert was doing or even why; many did not even notice the lighting changed. They just knew something was up (why else would there be a productivity guru in their midst...?) and were afraid of the changes this may bring about- In good human fashion, the possibility of demotion or termination of their own position, so the fear instilled in them resulted in their work becoming that much more efficient almost universally; on TWO occasions within days of each other.

Back to entertainment... An example of a perfectly executed advertising and promotional campaign utilizing a new media platform (at the time, of course) was the film "The Blair Witch Project" use of the internet as a marketing vehicle back in July of 1999. It was one of the first, if not the first, film to do so; certainly the first low-budget film to employ the internet and exploit it to it's fullest potential, given the time of course. This was not the only, but most certainly the most salient reason how this ultra low-budget horror film, made for a reported budget of $60,000 grossed $248,600,000. To clarify, that is $4,143.33 to every dollar invested, or an R.O.I. ("Return on Investment") of 414,333%.

Actually, and to keep myself honest, following the production itself, close to an additional million dollars were needed for post-production and to get the film to a decent enough quality so it can be exhibited theatrically in cinemas; and this was just prior to HD ("High Definition") being the norm... But you must admit, it is still a pretty monumental achievement nonetheless.

On the other end of the spectrum, in promoting a book recounting the belligerent sexual escapades of one Tucker Max, "I Hope they serve Beer in Hell", which reportedly sold just over 1.5 million copies and is now virtually a cult classic among college students, the author actually launched a campaign against the sexist and misogynistic nature of his own literary marvel (yes, I am being cynical in the unlikely event you were wondering...).

First, he agitated the delicate homeostasis of our very PC ("politically correct") society by provoking the public's ire and sense of self-righteousness in posting provocative, many times demeaning, banners both on line and utilizing physical billboards. Then, he "sought retribution" (from himself nonetheless...) by standing up, and coming out, against these insults on line, in billboards, by post cards and fliers.

This "faux" campaign worked wonders. It rallied feminists, sororities and a host of female support groups to propagate the book by the mere public discussion of it, thus elevating its online presence tremendously. Every demonstration or rally against the book contributed to its notoriety and kept it in the headlines and the public's eye. Not that I read the book, but from the little I know (not to mention the author's own admission), most of those 1.5 million books were sold because of the "noise", rather than the actual substance. A pig perhaps, but one damn clever swine for sure. This "false-positive" created by staging the initial "faux" counter-attack against the book and its author is quite often used in politics as well.

The scenario involving Russia's campaign leading to the annexation of the Crimean peninsula will be discussed later in a similar context, utilizing the same arsenal. Yes, IT IS all the same BS- Frightening perhaps, but true nonetheless.

In brainstorming, generating ideas for existing entities, goods or services or coming up with ideas for new companies, products, advertising and such, nothing is off the table. Thinking "outside the box" is not only encouraged, but required today. With so much advertising and marketing stimuli today, a new entity, product or marketing campaign must find a way to stand out from the crowd. In terms of new ideas, it is worth noting that throughout history, EVERY inventor or great thinker was ostracized at best; and burned at the stake at worst.

To paraphrase the astute George Bernard Shaw, *"Some people see the way things are and ask why? I see the way things should be and ask, why not?"*

I think about the following scenario on many occasions- What would my own reaction be if I were sitting among friends; just hanging out and socializing when one of them, out of the blue, said they had an idea for a service offering a discounted taxi services in their private vehicle to other strangers (Über, Lyft), or a service whereby one stranger would sub-let their main domicile to another (AirBNB, HomeAway)…? In all honesty, I'd most likely ask if they were professional crack heads, or if I could please have whatever it is they were smoking.

Recall those TV commercials that are most memorable to you for a moment. I'm sure you'll concur most took either a genius or madman (or madwoman) to conceive. Dos Equis' "Most Interesting Man in the World", Flo from Progressive, the Geico gecko, or those timeless Nike campaigns. Thinking about how the mind of these advertising geniuses' works, the age-old, but very perceptive adage, *"A creative adult is a child who survived"* comes to mind.

Mentioned briefly above, Star Wars is a great example embodying many of the topics covered herein- A relentless pursuit of passion and determination, a project made against all odds which almost everyone expected to fail and the foresight of thinking outside the box in terms of both the film and related revenue streams which never existed and no one recognized the potential of; except for one man, George Lucas.

Several years following the tremendous success of the coming of age film, American Graffiti (made for $777,000 and earning $140 million), George Lucas started making the Star Wars film, the most lucrative science-fiction film franchise in history. At the time, no one took sci-fi films seriously as the genre simply had too many flops. Released in 1977 over Memorial Day weekend, the first installment "A New Hope", shattered all expectations and grossed $775.4 million worldwide.

Believe it or not, that wasn't the genius foresight... Lucas reduced his directing fee by $500,000 in exchange for keeping all licensing and merchandising rights to himself. You see, not only was science-fiction a risky and overall undesirable genre to invest in, but merchandising film properties and licensing consumer goods from them was completely unheard of. Just as with the film itself, contrary to almost everyone's expectations, merchandising and licensing grew to become a cash cow never seen in Hollywood before, or since...

In 1978, 40 million "Star Wars" action figures sold grossing over $100 million. In 2011, a year in which there was no new "Star Wars" movie made, the franchise's merchandising brought in $3 billion...Then there are 33 years in between and the seven years since...

The Star Wars films show considerable similarity to both Roman mythology and Japanese "Jidaigeki" films; Japanese period dramas, usually from the Edo era. In fact, Lucas himself called the first installment an homage to the legendary Japanese director, Akira Kurosawa's "The Hidden Fortress". Genius attracts genius.

Ebert & Roeper's review of the film read as such...: "George Lucas has achieved what few artists do; he has created and populated a world of his own. His "Star Wars" movies are among the most influential, both technically and commercially, ever made". Quite an endorsement from two of the most noted film critics of the twentieth century.

With new ventures, new product or product line launches, promotional, marketing ad and PR campaigns, thinking outside the box has always been and will always remain absolutely vital for success. In many cases, it is the ability to foresee the value of something before anyone recognizes it. Just like Bugsy Siegel with Las Vegas- *"Build it and they will come..."*. No idea is too crazy that it cannot be a winner IF packaged and presented properly to the right audience and at the right time; within legal boundaries and societal norms of course...

Given that our threshold for excitement; whether it be Vegas hotels, casinos or resorts (or those of Dubai, Hong Kong, New York or any major metropolis for that matter), our insatiable appetite for consumer products or the same applied to our sexual escapades, drug consumption (not you, but society as a whole; more about that later), the video games we play, the music we listen to or the outdoor activities we participate in, it is only fitting that the envelope is being pushed strictly in one direction...

In the Aug/Sept 2017 issue of The Economist's "1843" periodical, the cover story discusses how some of Silicone Valley's top venture capitalists and billionaires consume micro doses of LSD to "open up" and be more creative; a claim long held by it's inventor; the first person to synthesize, ingest and learn of the psychedelic effects of lysergic acid diethylamide, the Swiss Dr. Albert Hofmann. Named one of the "100 Greatest Living Geniuses" of the 20th century and awarded many accolades, Dr. Hofmann often referred to LSD as his "problem child" (no shit...) and was resentful that the often reckless popularization of LSD by the American psychologist and writer, Timothy Leary, to his celebrity clientele during the 60's, discredited the drug's reputation and detracted from it's potential benefits.

Unfortunately, the propaganda ecosystem in which we all live has caused many other potentially beneficial attributes of certain drugs which they labeled as "Class A" (i.e., having no medicinal value under any circumstances or any merit/s whatsoever) from being discovered. Again, as illustrated with religion, the government too thinks we're too stupid to know (or too unreliable to handle) the truth.

Let's face it, most chances are you're not (I, for one, am certainly not...) a "Dean Kamen" (inventor of the Segway, the Auto Syringe insulin pump, the iBOT powered wheel chair, a game-changing water purification system named Slingshots and those push button Coke machines that offer a virtually endless array of beverage options...) or a "Lord James Dyson" (inventor of those game-changing air treatment and air purification appliances, commercial hand dryers, personal hair dryers and that vacuum cleaner you should make use of more often). That being the case, we need all the help we can get...

As illustrated by the above-referenced examples of Über, Lyft, AirBNB and HomeAway as well as those featured in the documentary "Something Ventured" noted before, the concept of thinking "outside the box" in Silicon Valley is of course not relegated to LSD consumption. Today, these young brash genius minds have adopted another philosophy to follow.

One of the most prolific figures of the twentieth
century who conceived what is now known as
Objectivism, was the Russian-American philosopher,
Ayn Rand (né Alisa Zinov'yena Rosenbaum). Also a
novelist, playwright and screenwriter, she wrote two
of the most influential (though quite voluminous)
novels of her time; "The Fountainhead" and "Atlas
Shrugged".

Today, some of the most successful and wealthiest
high tech titans point to Ayn Rand as the source of
their inspiration. She is one of the most admired
thinkers throughout Silicon Valley. Their favorite
quote of hers…? *"The question isn't who is going to let me;
it's who is going to stop me."* Remember, you have been
duly warned…

While having the technical know-how, these brazen
young kids developing our tomorrow lack a bit of life
experience and the wisdom it brings. At no time in
history did the young have such a grasp on the old
guard. Like everything else, this too presents both
positive and negative implications, but, when the
effects of the "work" can be immediately
disseminated across the globe instantaneously,
regardless if the "work" is a post, an image, an idea, a
product, a new social media platform, perhaps even
an "app" (while this referred to a tasty "appetizer" in
days past, today it of course carries a whole new,
completely tasteless, meaning), the results can be both
devastating and irreversible.

Such is the story of one Ross William Ulbricht, aka "Dread Pirate Roberts" (in tribute to the 80's film, "A Princess Bride"), founder of the modern day "Silk Road", but now in captivity for life. Fixated on the ostensible inconsistencies of how the U.S. government determined what was and what was not legal, his idea was simple: Create a black market on the dark net so that users would be able to peruse it anonymously and securely without traffic monitoring or oversight. The intention was to have a free and unscrutinized ecosystem for drug trade where the dealers would be rated, hence the drugs would be top shelf and the compensation would be paid by cryptocurrency, so that all will be safe and discreet.

The site launched in February, 2011, and, by all conventional measures, Mr. Ulbricht was helming a unicorn with a trajectory not unlike any of the other household names of his counterparts at the time, Über, AirBNB among others. As part of the dark web, the Silk Road operated as a Tor hidden service; the first completely anonymous and autonomous modern dark net market. Well, since Silk Road presented a means of trading anything to anyone with complete anonymity, it opened up a Pandora's Box that could not be tamed and cannot be undone.

Well beyond it's initial raison d'être, the Silk Road was quickly discovered by human traffickers who auctioned people they abducted as sex slaves and by terrorists who purchased weapons and other arsenal to wage their battles. That being the case, in October of 2013, the FBI shut down Silk Road and arrested Ulbricht. As a close friend once told me about my own path, "The road to hell is paved with good intentions". As stated, he is now incarcerated for life without parole, but Silk Road "2.0" came back online less than a month after being shut down- On November 6, 2013. God help us all- "*In a mad world, only the mad are sane*" as the immensely talented Japanese film director, Akira Kurosawa, once said.

History is laden with "genius regret". No one knows what something will morph into, how certain discoveries will ultimately be used and for what will inventions intended for one application also be appropriate to serve. The conundrum of Frankenstein, but this is reality and it has consequences. That statement above about good intentions and hell, about turning back time or pushing the "reset" or "clear" button.

Some regretful folks who invented things for one purpose, which was ultimately, perhaps even primarily, used for another quite different purpose, include the following (and this, most definitely, is a partial list): Alfred Nobel invented TNT for mining purposes; it ended up killing more people than any other single invention of mankind. Albert Einstein split atoms with nuclear fission in order to create energy; instead, his discovery led to the proliferation of the nuclear race which defined the Cold War and may still spell our demise, depending on whether Mr. Kim or Mr. Trump mature one day or just remain two juvenile delinquents driven by their ego with the future of humanity hanging in the balance, but we digress...

William Powell, who published "The Anarchist Cookbook" back in 1970 at the ripe age of 19, has gone so far as to make a film to serve as a testament of his regret ("American Anarchist"- to be found on Netflix as well). John Sylvan, inventor of the coffee pod regrets inventing it due to the pollution it causes, not to mention it contributing to an already addictive society, by lamenting that his pods are "... like a cigarette for coffee- a single sleeve delivery for an addictive substance". Bob Propst is sorry for the inhumane treatment of workers his office cubicle causes Mikhail Kalashnikov is aghast with the number of lives lost to his eponymous rifle and the AK-47 (though he HAD to know that guns kill people. Sorry! People kill people, but the gun certainly helps... As my favorite British comedian, Eddie Izzard, pointed out to everyone's astonishment.

Lastly, even Sean Parker has expressed remorse at what Facebook morphed into, how much time it consumes from people's lives and what damage it inflicts on their social skills as well as humanity overall. It takes genuine maturity to express such remorse, but I suspect the billions made in the interim helped Mr. Parker a bit... Nonetheless, the fact that a recent survey found that FB users spend 50 minutes a day interacting on the social network compounded by the fact that, as of the third calendar quarter or 2017, the site had 2.07 billion monthly active users, easily quantify the "opportunity cost" in a dollar amount. If these people would all get paid just the minimum wage (at a company with 26+ employees) at the prevailing rate of $12/hour in 2017, the dollar figure of said opportunity cost amounts to over $20 billion each day. And that's JUST Facebook…

Attributed to both Saint Benedict of Nurcia and Saint Francis of Assisi, there is a perfect passage which explains the feeling of such "genius regret", in following adage: *"More tears have been shed over answered prayers than unanswered ones"*. Whichever it was of the two, well said indeed… Bottom line- Be careful what you wish for.

Next is learning- Improving and advancing to become the very best you can be in any endeavor you choose. I am in the concept of *"Kaizen"* (a Japanese philosophy which means *"perpetual learning"*- The concept that, no matter what you do (as a profession, in business or for leisure), it can always be improved and made better by continuous learning, observation and experimentation; i.e., that one should never stop studying). This philosophy made it big in the American corporate ecosystem circa 1980's guised as some abstract ancient Japanese "secret", which, of course, it is not. Like most things in life, it's just logic and deductive reasoning; pure and simple.

One of my closest mentors and friends, about 60 years my senior, Dr. Bakshi, God rest his soul, a much revered holistic Indian doctor from London, taught me the concept of "Kaizen"; not by name, rather, by practice. This man knew more about physics than an M.I.T. professor, more about Catholic doctrines than a Cardinal and more about coffee than Juan Valdez. No, really.

So…Learn. Learn about anything and everything that interests you personally or could benefit you professionally. For example, not only completion courses for doctors introducing them to new medicines, prognosis techniques, information about certain ailments (their possible cause/s, symptom/s and/or treatment options), or similarly for surgeons, teachers and so forth.

It is important to always remember the timeless Chinese proverb, *"Give a man a fish, and you feed him for a day. Teach a man to fish, and you feed him for a lifetime"*.

You should also be as cognizant and observant as possible, thus learning not only from the masters of ancient and contemporary thought and invention, such as; Homer, Laozi, Confucius, Darius, Heraclitus, Socrates, Hippocrates, Plato, Aristotle, Al-Farabi, Avicenna, Rashi, Averroes, The Rambam, Nostradamus, Galileo, Leonardo da Vinci, Benjamin Franklin, Alexander Hamilton, Victor Hugo, Ralph Waldo Emerson, Charles Darwin, Abraham Lincoln, Charles Dickens, Henry David Thoreau, Mark Twain, Friedrich Nietzsche, Oscar Wilde, Nikola Tesla, Mahatma Gandhi, Albert Einstein, Franz Kafka, Jean-Paul Sartre, Alan Turing, Nelson Mandela, Gore Vidal, Thich Nhat Hanh, Elie Wiesel, Martin Luther King, Chinua Achebe, The Dalai Lama, or Stephen Hawking, but also from benign culprits like your children, your hairdresser or bartender, even your pet. EVERYONE knows something you don't and, sharing their teachings, memories, experiences and lessons learned will contribute, at some level and in some capacity,

Side note: If, by some unforeseen happenstance, you do not recognize any go the above-listed names, it would most definitely behoove you to research, perhaps even study, them and their genius and contributions to humanity a tad bit.

The bottom line is the almost any person we encounter, every place we visit and almost every interaction we experience can contribute to molding and, ultimately, making you the very best you can be.

As I hope you'll see in the coming pages, I myself learned greatly from my stepson, my own children, even my pets and almost everyone I have ever met and everything I experienced in my life thus far. No shit.

To augment your never-ending learning experience, your own "Kaizen" should consist not only of seminars, completion courses and keeping up with your developments and advancements in your field of expertise or scope of work, but, whenever you stumble across a word you do not recognize, look it up. Do the same when you encounter historical or current events, people, quotes and proverbs you are unaware of. Trust me, at some point, that knowledge will come in handy. Just as importantly, it will keep you relevant and "in the know"- VERY important in today's labor market, not to mention with your kids.

So, remain curious and inquisitive, ask questions and research what matters or interests you (or that to which you have no answer AND want to know). If you continuously examine, investigate and experiment, you will benefit yourself, your surroundings, maybe even all of us somehow. Benjamin Franklin wittingly noted: "*Life's tragedy is that we get old too soon and wise too late*".

This practice will open your mind, present different ways and solutions to the challenges life presents and problems you encounter along the way. Besides, then you'll understand what it means to say: "...*those who think they know everything, bother those of us who really do*."

Lastly on the topic of learning: Up to only a few decades ago, our knowledge of the brain was quite minimal- We knew it was quite important so we didn't screw with it too much; just as the Hippocratic Oath promises: "*primum non nocere*", or "*first, do no harm*". It is only with the advent of the CAT Scan and MRI machines that we started learning about that brain of ours we hardly use; quite a bit in fact. So much so that today we can decipher thoughts with the use of electrodes as conduits and the still-in-progress mapping of the brain. Few have followed this progress as close as Mr. Michio Kaku, a Japanese-American theoretical physicist professor and, if you want to know anything about the space between your ears, you must read his "The Future of the Mind". Truly amazing work.

In commerce there is a triangle represented by time, quality and price. It is known that only two of the three angles are available at any time- If you need something quickly, it will most likely be costlier than the norm and quality will inevitably suffer, even if slightly. If you have the time to get a project executed properly, it's quality will most likely improve and it won't cost an arm and a leg. You see, it's either a buyer's or seller's market. It is the very basic law of economics as well- That of supply and demand.

And, never forget- In most cases, you get what you pay for; one way or the other.

An example of this very basic, but omnipresent, law in all commerce- Need to liquidate assets quickly? Like sell a car or some baseball cards…? If you're in a rush, you won't obtain the best price possible. Just like getting a room in a Las Vegas hotel on New Year's Eve right cost $1,000, but come January 2, the same room will most likely cost a fraction of that price.

Also concerning pricing or the traditional MSRP ("Manufacturers Suggested Retail Price"), there are formulas to derive what that price should be based on the COGS ("Cost of Goods Sold"). In very broad terms (because this is not an economic book), the more units of a particular good you sell and other factors, such as the easier, or less costly (both in terms of time and cost), it is to get these products to market (i.e., for end-user consumption), the lower the profit margin needs to be. The less units you sell, the higher the margin needs to be.

The other big variable here is the actual price of the commodity in question because, naturally, 20% of a Subway salad varies just a tad from 20% of a Rolls Royce Phantom. That is supply-side economics- i.e., what something should cost the consumer based on it's COGS, or manufacturing costs, transportation costs (air, ship, truck or, soon, drone and whether the item is fungible or perishable thus needing refrigeration; all of which need to get factored in) and, of course, an allowance for the retailer selling the product (perhaps also a distributor between the manufacturer and retailer, or even a few brokers along the way), to make their margin, or profit, as well (are you beginning to see why Amazon was such a brilliant idea, in so many ways...?). This is supply-side economics.

By the way, this is why consolidation always happens, as we will re-visit later citing the automotive, music and mass merchant industries as examples, of this phenomenon. Consolidation enables companies to streamline operations, operate with less people than if they were to operate independently and enjoy economies of scale (lowered raw materials and production/ manufacturing costs based of sheer size).

This is why a Subway can beat any "mom & pop" sandwich shop, or an Office Depot any family-owned stationery store. So, while we all enjoy those unbelievably low prices a Walmart, just remember they do come at a great cost- Both to the entrepreneurial spirit that is the foundation of all free market economies, not to mention, the American psyche, as well as to those manufacturers that get squeezed so very, very much and for whom even the slightest miscalculation (or natural disaster or a number of other small variables outside their control), could spell absolute disaster.

On the other side is demand-side economics. How desired is the product, by how many people and at what price. For example, if we have a lip stick to sell, how many people will buy that li stick at $5/unit and how many will at $10/unit- This is referred to as "price flexibility". These reasons are precisely why we need those selling "hook/s" for our products and where their marketing and promotion come into play most. To convince people we have the very best product and, by creating (or inflating, in many cases) it's true value to create what is known as "perceived" value so consumers believe it is most certainly worth what we are asking them to pay.

People willing to pay $8,000 for a Hermès Birkin bag, not to mention a wait of three+ years, (last year one actually sold for $185,000 on eBay), both mean that bag has a tremendous appeal (i.e., a very high perceived value) to consumers and enjoys great price flexibility (as there are few other bags in this world that could sell at that price). This, of course, is not to say they could not sell more of these bags at $1,000, but that is not their market nor what the luxury brand market is about. It is about exclusivity which can only be present with scarcity. Yup, just like those diamonds mentioned above.

By the way, sorry for mentioning the price of the bag-
As the magnate Andrew Carnegie noted: "*If you need to
ask how much it is, you probably cannot afford it*" and, of
course, I mean no disrespect…

Price flexibility is such an important, all too often
overlooked, aspect of determining a product's MSRP,
I want to illustrate just how delicate it is. In my mid-
20's, we sold VHS cassettes of various motorsports
content through televised direct marketing campaigns.
We were selling a two-tape set (the actual program
plus a "giveaway" tape) at $29.95, plus S&H
("Shipping & Handling"). The product was great,
people liked it, but it just wasn't moving. We sold
about two thousand sets in our first year and barely
broke even given the commercial time we purchased,
as minimal as it was…

The following year, we reduced the price to $19.95
plus S&H, and split one of the two tapes into a
double-cassette set (with the giveaway tape now being
the third), hence made the physical appearance of the
product appear more "robust", thus increasing it's
perceived value compared to the old packaging. The
combination of the lowered price point and
heightened perceived value gave my family it's first
real financial windfall in the United States, but don't
ask what happened next… By the way, obviously the
lowered price had significantly more to do with sales
being successful than the higher perceived value of
the product with it's new, three-VHS cassette set up.

Most similar products were in fact priced at $19.95 so that was the "natural" price point for the "Crash Impact" trilogy we sold.

Any company's "goodwill" is that intangible value placed on it's brand awareness, consumer loyalty and product identity. What makes it a successful enterprise and what makes it stand out from the pack (or it's competitors). Nowhere are these more prevalent and apparent than with, of course, Coca Cola (until they brought us New Coke, way back in April, 1985, "...A day that will live in infamy". Sorry, no disrespect, that was phrase was of course made after the attacks on Pearl Harbor, but, in terms of the beverage industry, the phrase could have very well been adopted in Coke's case... Further proof that, "... if it ain't broke, don't fix it".).

Since neither you nor I own Coca Cola, in our world, goodwill manifests itself in two ways; return and referral business. If someone is a plumber and has been for many years (and provided he/she is a decent plumber and an honest man or woman) and does not need to advertise or promote his/her business to sustain it, the repeat and return business the plumber receives can be construed and quantified easily as his/her goodwill. If you are looking to buy the business, of course you need to add the equipment, supplies and raw materials, if any, on top of it's goodwill to determine it's fair market value.

This notion is equally prevalent in the concept of licensing (and, in the exact opposite manner, but same logic, white labeling). It is the belief that a brand name will being about one or both of the following results: First, it should cater a product and make it appealing to an already existing clientele or specific consumer market segment that both identifies and has an affinity for the brand name being licensed. Second, if it is an upscale or luxury brand, it should elevate a product's perceived value if presented/ packaged under that particular brand name.

In many cases, a brand is so well respected and /or recognized, it becomes a very fruitful revenue source and, after operations cease, the only surviving financial stream. Take for example Playboy's iconic bunny logo- For the better part of the last few decades of that company pror to it being sold, it's licensing has been the best money generator in terms of profit margin for that lifestyle brand.

Other notable examples of those exploiting their own brands from a licensing perspective are Christian Audigier licensing his now defunct "Ed Hardy" to virtually every consumer product class in existence, the longevity and wide distribution of products branded under the band KISS by Gene Simmons who somehow manages to keep it relevant decades following the end of its recording life, and the genius of Jimmy Buffett who virtually built a lifestyle empire based on a single hit, "Magrgaritaville".

Later we'll discuss charitable giving, the donating of both money and time, anonymously and eponymously, but we should touch on the subject, from the perspective of a company's image and it's standing in the community. Charity adds quite a bit, so much so in fact that there has been a paradigm shift in how corporate America views, and utilizes, charitable giving.

Just as the local coffee shop supporting a neighborhood cause or a small business donating to the regional Little League, elevates both their visibility in the local community, buying a pair of shoes from Tom's knowing another pair will be given for free to someone in need, makes you, the consumer, feel better about buying a pair of shoes from them.

Founded in 1982 by actor Paul Newman and author A.E. Hotchner, Newman's Own is a food company that gives 100% of it's after tax profits to the Newman's Own Foundation. When evaluating competitive products in the same price range, I, as a consumer, would opt to buy this product given the ultimate use of my money at the end of the day (my mother would do the same, but most likely due to the fact the packaging features an illustration of Mr. Newman, one of her favorite actors).

Establish a common denominator with your clients and potential customers. I used to produce and sell television (and video, when that was a thing...) programs around the world. As such, I made it a point to know something about every country and each culture so I could establish a (albeit basic) rapport & create a dialogue with my existing clients and potential customers. It made the small talk matter and created a bond through familiarity, or a seeming familiarity and added a personal angle to an to an otherwise wry business exchange.

Epiphany- Such a lovely word and so enlightening. You never know when it will strike and how long you'll be able to remember or recreate the exact look, wording or appearance of whatever it is you thought of. True, epiphanies tend to appear at the most inconvenient times- During gridlock, in the shower, on the crapper (named so after it's inventor, really...), during foreplay, or right before dozing off to sleep. Much like dreams, these ideas come quickly and disappear just as fast, so my advice is to do what I do- Have mankind's greatest inventions, the Post It and the pen with me at all times and everywhere- The pocket of my jeans, by my bed and in my car. This, by the way, is how this book was first conceived; with approximately $200 worth of Post-Its to be exact (not that you asked).

Although it may seem as an exercise in futility, writing down your thoughts, ideas, aspirations and goals is also a worthwhile practice to adopt. These notes represent a visual (and physical) testament to thought, which is of course intangible. Doing so basically transforms an abstract idea to a material document- A short journey from fantasy to reality, that can't be bad...

It is important to have these items within reach at all times, at least in my experience, because you never know when genius strikes; and you don't know how long it'll last (we've all had thoughts or dreams we swore we would remember and be able to recall, only to find out otherwise just moments later when the spark mysteriously dissipated into oblivion). This is akin to a light bulb that illuminates instantaneously, but is gone in a flash...

...And remember, "*If your dreams don't scare you, they're not big enough*".

That is why I recommend to be ready at all times with these essential utensils; just like that gun, knife, mace, pepper spray or tazer in the event of an intruder or flashlight in the event of a natural disaster or power outage by the side of your bed.

Another thought about the world of writing and chronicling- This one more therapeutic in nature. Another seemingly fruitless habit of scribing, is to do so to those who have maliciously hurt, defamed, harmed, slandered, humiliated or otherwise agitated you. Even if the letter (or email or post) never reach the culprit, this practice provides significant healing for some unknown reason; as if a burden has been lifted.

Besides, having a written physical (or digital...) record will free up some mind as well as decrease the level of anxiety and stress you endure so that your brain is vacated, your energies are restored and able to focus elsewhere; hopefully, on a more productive use of these resources and for a more beneficial purpose.

Since you are in a scribing mode, another practice I find essential to properly evaluate and arrive at the correct decision is to list the pros and cons of any important choice to be made or pivotal option to be selected. You must read through the jargon, look beyond the words and listen past the noise to extract people's true meaning and real intention, so that clarity prevails and is present when a course of action is chosen.

Like life itself, each crossroad is an enigma, but it is best deciphered by a simple balance sheet weighing the positives and negatives of all viable options.

One more thought on the subject- Don't ever just "assume"; seek clarity- *"If you "assume", you make an "ass" of "u" and "me".*

Just as mentioned above, once the deliberation is over and a choice has been made, immediately pursue it with resolute fervor and absolute passion; and do it with extreme zeal and never ever stop until you reach your goal and very own Eureka.

By the way, this is true whether you're pursuing a goal or courting a mate you wish to charm (or, conversely, hunting down an adversary). Equally, these need to be pursued with relentless vigor and such an overwhelming manner that, once done, either the goal is attained, the heart of that whom you desire is captured or, in the case of your nemesis, strike swiftly, with precision and be fatal in delivery- Like the swoosh of a Samurai's katana or the bite of a cobra's fangs; right to the jugular.

My apologies in advance, but as this passage perfectly captures the spirit of this swift and lethal approach, I must insert a short monologue from Quentin Tarantino's 1994 neo-noir masterpiece, "Pulp Fiction". Delivered so majestically by Samuel Jackson's "Jules Winnfield" character (and, no, it is not the same verbiage to that of the scripture text quoted from Ezekiel 25:17, as professed in the film) and delivered each time just before taking another man's life, it reads the following:

*"The path of the righteous man is beset on all sides by the
inequities of the selfish and the tyranny of evil men. Blessed is
he who, in the name of charity and good will, shepherds the
weak through the valley of the darkness, for he is truly his
brother's keeper and the finder of lost children."*

*"And I will strike down upon thee with great vengeance and
furious anger those who attempt to poison and destroy my
brothers. And you will know I am the Lord when I lay my
vengeance upon you."*

Next on the agenda: Conduct brainstorming sessions
with like minds. Whatever it is you're involved in,
there should be a brain trust that you can and should
consult with from time to time. This is of course
applies to new endeavors. This is how some of the
greatest ideas and most successful "unicorns" (a term
which describes $1billion+ tech start-ups) were
conceived; Uber was thought of at a rainy Paris
apartment for one and, Solar City, one of the
predominant solar panel companies in the U.S. was
first suggested by Elon Musk (yes, he is
EVERYWHERE…) to his cousins, Lyndon & Peter
Rive in 2004 on the way to AND go, at least once in
your lifetime).

Communal brainstorming is far from being a new
concept. It is in fact responsible for most inventions,

innovations and ideas for new businesses. It was practiced by ancient thinkers in Greece, artists in Firenze (Florence) during the Italian "Rinascimento" ("Renaissance" or "Re-birth"), at Bohemian salons of 19th Century Saint Germain des Prés in Paris, at avant-garde art galleries in Greenwich Village, the now renowned "Lunch Group" of OG venture capitalists in 60's San Francisco, the annual Davos Summit resulting from the 1971 founding of the World Economic Forum by Klaus Schwab, the more shadowy Bohemian Grove or Freemason organizations, Harvard's Porcellian Club and other alma mater associations as well as think tank organizations such as the Brookings Institution, RAND Corporation, Council on Foreign Relations, The Heritage Foundation, the Center for Strategic and International Studies, Cato Institute, the Carnegie Endowment for International Peace and so forth…

The point here was not to pollute your eyes with a list of organizations, but to underscore both the contribution and continuing importance of "communal thought" or a "thought collective"- From the "council of elders" comprised of wise sages in tribal societies or those enterprises listed above in today's   age.

4 INTERACTION UNDER DURESS, IDENTIFYING DECEIT & SUBTERFUGE, BATTLING HOSTILITY AND CONFRONTING SABOTAGE

As a precursor to this section, there are two very simple yet indispensable books you need to read- Sun Tzu's "The Art of War" and Niccolò Machiavelli's "The Prince". Both basically list the doctrines and protocol to follow en route to ruling the world; a roadmap for Dr. Evil, if you will. Such life lessons as the former's: "... *Keep your friends close and your enemies closer*" and "*To make your enemy a friend, create a problem for them, then solve it*" and so forth.

To start with, "*the first rule on any game is to know you're in one*", so keep your eyes and ears open and always remain alert to identify the situation you are presently in; whether by choice or by force.

A little personal interjection here- From my own observations, I believe there are two types of people in this world- Those that are inherently good and those that are inherently bad. Those that are givers and those that are takers. Those that are enlightened and those still finding their way in the dark. Those who are elevated and those still trapped beneath the surface. We can try to teach and show the way to those lost souls, but, just like that horse from the very beginning of our journey, we cannot make them drink from the well. Also interesting to note is the distinct difference between those who "create", who tend be happy, giving people to those who "consume", who tend to be quite the opposite; usually unhappy with a sense of entitlement.

Resulting from the above, not to mention many other reasons cited thus far (with more to come…), it is absolutely imperative to be cautious and very, very careful in whom we entrust power, for power in the wrong hands can be devastating, even fatal. Just look back at history- World history as well as that of your own. Whenever power is in the wrong hands, its abuse is rampant and boundless. Unchecked and without consequence, this abuse will only grow in severity, even outright cruelty."… *Power corrupts; absolute power corrupts absolutely*" a notion voiced by John Dalberg, the 1st Baron of Acton which we will re-visit soon. It illustrates just how intoxicating, corrosive and addictive power is and where it can lead.

An important piece of advice is to side with caution; in all forms. A derivative of this notion is "*to know AND respect thy enemy*". The Vietnam War was a lost cause for many reasons: In many cases, we just couldn't tell who was an enemy combatant and who was an ally. Second, an armed soldier pictured next to a woman, child, an elderly or disabled person can never win in the court of public opinion (but that usually static image was much more scarce in those days compared to today's constant & simultaneous audiovisual coverage of any global battlefront; with both images and video, providing both a visual and an audio record of the events as they unfold in real time).

In this sordid war, from a purely strategic vantage point, the United States failed in recognizing the Viet Cong's superior knowledge of jungle warfare; in terms of logistical support & accessibility, navigating the terrain and ability to replenish supplies. Beyond these, the benefits of camouflage the jungle embodies were also advantageous only to our adversaries, not to mention the sweltering humidity matched only by Biloxi, Mississippi.

Finally, but of paramount importance and relevance, is the value of human life. There is a rather morose ranking of human life in terms of a monetary valuation in different countries at specific times. In real terms, that means if advancing one hundred yards in a battlefield is estimated to cost the lives of a dozen soldiers, how easily will the commanding officer give the order to go forth. In this war, the disparity was glaring.

It is imperative to remember that: *"Cultures don't divide people; values do"*.

The same notion was conveyed half way across the world, in another dispute, but at the same period of time, by Prime Minister Golda Meir when she poignantly noted that; *"Peace will come when the Arabs will love their children more than they hate us."*

As discussed, toxic people fall into two major categories in terms of the main locomotive driving their decisions and actions. The first are deceitful people who essentially go through life screwing and sabotaging others for their livelihood. The second are those who are driven by their ego. You should avoid these two groups at all costs and keep them as far from your heart, business or family at any cost. That said, both groups feature the identical personality traits in terms of narcissism, being self-centered, arrogant with an all-too boisterous sense of entitlement. And, yes, most have a low sense of both self-worth and self-esteem and, more often than not, even hate themselves.

Don't get me wrong- Ego is good. It gives us a sense of our own self-worth and places a value on our time, talent/s, idea/s, contribution and work. That said, EVERYTHING in moderation of course. Like any addiction, enslavement by one's ego is no different. If not curbed properly, just like any narcotic, it will become thirstier and crave more stimuli to be

placated. And, with each instance, more damage will
be inflicted- On co-workers, friends and even family
members. Yes, just as with drugs, ego hath no
friends…

The benefit of an inflated ego to rest of humanity is
that, most often, it is what ultimately brings about the
downfall of the person and unmasks the callous mind
it controls. You see, precisely because of their ego,
these narcissists tend to be exceedingly arrogant; so
much so that they cannot control themselves and
must gloat and boast endlessly to feed that ego of
theirs, but, at the same time, they often inadvertently
reveal what are their true intentions and the real
identity behind the veil. Vanity is indeed an expensive
hobby.

Returning to those deceitful people mentioned above,
be leery of charlatans- If it sounds too good to be
true, it probably is. In my view, everyone is suspect
until proven otherwise (notice, I said "suspect", not
"guilty"). Hence, adopt President Theodore
Roosevelt's philosophy towards foreign policy; "*Speak
softly, but carry a big stick*".

Coined during the Vietnam War, the term "fugazi"
(or, "fugazy") came to mean "fake" or "counterfeit",
as vividly animated by the Mark Hannah character in
"Wolf of Wall Street". Although not Italian in origin,
some suspect it's a derivative of the Italian term

"fugace" which means "fleeting" or "impermanent". In short, BULLSHIT, fiction, an illusion, a fraud, figment of one's imagination, a fantasy...

Just like pyramid sales, "robbing Peter to pay Paul", whatever... You don't have to be fooled by the maestro of Ponzi schemes, Bernie Madoff. I'm certain that somewhere along the line you've encountered a situation where someone assured that the next deal, stock tip or sales quarter revenue increase is a "sure thing". Be mindful, be careful- Do your own investigation and analysis and reach your own conclusions.

If you did make a mistake and only realized it post-facto, you must put an end to that relationship; IMMEDIATELY. Remember: *"Fuck me once, shame on you; fuck me twice, shame on me"*.

Just as is the case with making the wrong assessment of people the first time, but learning from your mistake, thus never repeating it, the same applies for an erroneous chosen MO- The definition of insanity (or stupidity) is doing the same thing twice, but expecting a different result each time. If you got screwed or a bad result the first time, do not repeat the action expecting a different consequence; it ain't coming...

"Hindsight is 20/20" (or"6/6" if metric is your
preferred measurement system...), but it provides no
benefit if you do not implement that which you have
learned from previous mistakes or misjudging.

Mark your territory- If someone oversteps their
boundary at work, with your wife or teenage
daughter, put them on check and nip it in the butt.
You don't have to be rude or demeaning, but be
stern, assertive and make absolutely certain to draw a
line in the sand; and one you will not allow to be
breached.

Stand your ground- Do not for one minute tolerate
an attempt at sabotage, insubordination, subterfuge,
thievery, fraud, embezzlement, cheating, lying or any
other nefarious, sinister or malicious plots.

A crime that goes unpunished will be repeated; in
many cases, in a much more extreme form. Devoid of
retribution, the perpetrator will also rationalize, even
justify, their actions. As such, all sinister plots must be
completely destroyed before they blossom and all
nefarious actions must be punished; "*An eye for an eye*".

Accountability is why every society abides by a set of
rules, every institution dictates a code of conduct and
every profession sets forth a protocol that all
members must respect and abide by. Attorneys have

the Bar Association, doctors the American Medical Association and so forth. Even the Cosa Nostra (mafia) has a set standard set of rules that guide behavior and action. Believe it or not, even the Armenians have the same concept called "orenk" that means precisely that...

In essence, the rule of law is the idea that every man/woman is held accountable for his/her actions and that these actions have consequences.

Those people with a low sense of self-esteem and worth, those who know they have little or no talent and ride on others' ideas and their execution, those who take credit for others' hard work... and so on, need to elevate their standing, their morale and their confidence and validate who they are and what they do by doing just that- By making others feel bad, dismissing and mocking them and all that they do. Beyond taking credit away from others, they also exaggerate their own actions, work and contribution. Left unchecked, they also lie; and cheat; and steal... It's simple; it's human nature. No dignity, no integrity, no loyalty, no morality, no ethics. *"What's yours is mine; what's mine is mine."*

A truly worthwhile hour spent on the subject is watching bestselling author and professor, Dan Ariely's award-winning documentary

"(DIS)HONESTY- The Truth About Lies" (yup, another gem; also on Netflix).

From time to time, every dog needs to get a rapid, vigorous pull-back of the leash so it stays on course and knows it's place. EVERYONE needs to get "checked" (reminded of their place, how they should behave and adjust erratic thoughts that may culminate in chaos; as is clearly the case here…). By "everyone" I mean precisely that- every employee, every friend, every child, husband or wife; shit, even the Pope and the President of the United States (that is why we have "checks & balances" between the Executive, Judicial and Legislative branches in the U.S. government. You know what happens in countries or times when we do not have this concept of "checks & balances" and power is left unchecked- Power mongering and corruption. Both of which stifle progress, growth and, of course, equality. This will be embellished on later.

As noted above, power corrupts. It is a very simple concept- It is intoxicating, corrosive and addictive. It causes people to believe their own PR & BS (VERY related acronyms) to an extent that could prove damaging to those who surround them as well as innocent bystanders and detrimental to themselves. They believe they live in an insulated cocoon or bubble rendering them untouchable by mortal edicts or code of conduct. Simply put, it fosters delusions of grandeur and a false feeling of being invincible and above the law.

But, Karma is a bitch and "*the bigger they are, the harder they fall…*". At the time of scribing this book, it has been just over two years since onset of when about three dozen women spoke out and accused Bill Cosby of sexual assault of a most heinous nature; drugging, then raping them while they were helplessly incapacitated. Today, we are in the midst of a tsunami of allegations against some of the most powerful icons in Hollywood and the entertainment industry in general; with a few politicians thrown in for good measure- Generally speaking (and this is an understatement of epic proportions), neither group has historically performed in stellar fashion on the spectrums of either ethical behavior or moral conduct.

This latest tidal wave exploded in the first week of October, 2017 with sexual misconduct allegations made against film mogul, Harvey Weinstein, in an appalling scandal culminating with over one hundred accusers within weeks; ranging in severity from sexual assault to outright rape, then tormenting and menacing his victims. It seems the producer of some of the finest and most rewarded films of the past three decades was moonlighting as an insidious serial rapist afflicting a substantial sliver of Hollywood's leading ladies and it's debutants in those same thirty long years. A modern-day Marquis de Sade. But Weinstein's demise was only the start.

#MeToo became a call for victims to come forth leading to a torrential barrage of empowered victims rising from their feeble shelters of silence to speak out and bring forth an onslaught of monumental downfalls and a barrage of firings from the forefront of society's apex. Respected anchormen whom we welcomed into our living rooms, actors of insurmountable talent, revered celebrity chefs, career politicians, acclaimed writers, respected journalists, brilliant comedians, a creator of a children's show, a top public radio editor and the eminent public television talk show host- ALL household names; and ALL collapsed in the face of truth.

This episode was as eye opening and reminiscent of the pedophilia-laden sexual scandals of the Catholic Church that plagued, but were largely covered-up until they started to sporadically surface in the 1980's. By the 1990's, the cases begun to receive significant media and public attention, but the church cried foul on the grounds of excessive and disproportionate coverage. A collection of television exposés, such as Ireland's "Suffer the Children" led to more scrutiny in many countries and attentive investigations commenced in that country as well as other European nations, the United States, Australia and Canada during those years.

A critical investigation in 2002 by The Boston Globe's Matt Carroll, Sacha Pfeiffer and Michael Rezendes, with editor Walter V. Robinson, which was the basis for the 2015 film "Spotlight", shed light on not only the rampant abuse, but, even more disturbing, the cover-ups. These were achieved by personal criminal threats, pay-offs to victims, sudden sabbaticals certain predatory clergy were sent on or the shuttling of priests from one parish to another so they are out of the limelight and locale of their accusers (but, in the latter case, were presented a new selection of prey to torment, disgusting).

From 2001 to 2010, the Holy See, the central governing body of the Catholic Church received sex abuse allegations against 3,000 or so priests dating back fifty years, with most occurring between 1960 and 1984. It is virtually impossible to quantify the devastation due to the grim   fact that the average time it took between being a victim of Catholic sexual abuse and seeking redress is 33 years. That is an entire lifetime; and to think these are the people we rely on to teach and safeguard our children. As the old Arab adage goes: *"Every dog has it's day…"*.

Back to our nemesis… In order to avert attention and, in many cases, succeed in avoiding retribution as a result of their less than desirable conduct, even crimes and lies, the notion that "the latest, most immediate and pertinent issues always dwarf the important issues"…. They essentially create an unrelated diversion, thus casting the spotlight at it. A perfect illustration of such a diversion tactic is the subject of the film "Wag the Dog".

Also used to divert one's attention or to simply take their time away from worthwhile endeavors is manipulating them or a situation so they focus somewhere else, usually engaged in some pointless task, futile exercise or meaningless work (under the guise of doing something of value or of necessity, of course) in order to have them waste their time and resources.

A book entitled "Without Sky", written by a renowned Russian political strategist and a chief architect of the Kremlin's propaganda machine, Vladislav Kurkov. In it, he illustrates how to create a faux-negative narrative (or positive, as needed...) or "aura" around a premise, idea or action by doing exactly the opposite- Creating false support for the cause at hand; much the same as was practiced in the annexation of Crimea when Russian nationals were "planted" there, as were many of the supposed Russian "loyalists" in the region were (essentially embedding a completely hidden fighting force with the Ukrainian population). By the way, demographic manipulation by populating disputed or unstable regions with citizens of the "mother (or "conquering") country". The same course is practiced by the Chinese in Tibet as well as the Myanmar government in the ruthless persecution and now genocidal campaign against the Rohingya people.

In "selling" their narrative, people also employ different occasions and "vehicles" (other people) to convey the specific message over and over until becomes "familiar" (or believed) by it's intended audience; also often used in politics; and at work... But, as Franklin D Roosevelt noted; "repetition does not transform a lie into a truth."

In politics, this is collectively termed "spin"- Spinning, or manipulating, the truth or facts to suit whatever narrative you want to support or present. It is no wonder why political strategists are quite often referred to as "Spin Doctors".

In a behavioral study, when asked how many times people who don't understand what a politician said (whether because he was outright bullshitting or it just sounded good- you know the recipe; big words, strong voice, powerful delivery, assertive demeanor, whatever...), pretend they actually did understand, believe and did not question neither the words, nor the authority of the message; the answer was a resounding 40+%.... With someone you "trust" (a confidant, a partner, anyone in your inner circle/s), that figure is of course far greater.

Mark Twain summed all of the above quite cleverly, as he often does, with these words: "*It ain't what you don't know that gets you in trouble; it's what you know that just isn't so*".

Another misnomer is "*The enemy of my enemy is my friend*". Not so much. I would much rather heed Thomas Jefferson's advice "*Beware entangling alliances*". Three words that mean so very much- Be careful who you befriend or align yourself with. When the United States unwittingly supported the Mujahideen of Afghanistan simply because they fought the Soviets, it was an alliance born of seeming necessity but was equally short-lived. You see, the Mujahideen morphed into the tyrannical Taliban who ruled Afghanistan according to the strict doctrines of Shari'a Law in it's devout (and quite literal) interpretation & application (to top this off, as is often the case when despots rule, a hearty dose of hypocrisy; as expected for those who rule with absolute power devoid of scrutiny). They plundered, pillaged and raped. They literally created a country of solitary confinement for women who had no rights and no liberties. They did not study, they could not drive and, at times, they simply died because a man was not allowed to lay his hands on them, even if it meant saving their life.

From this righteous blissful group of bearded zealots, adorned in their traditional shalwar kameez, and with the aid of one Osama bin Laden, a real estate developer (sounds familiar...?), the infamous Al Qaeda came to be. This took place just over twenty years after the United States armed, many times even trained, their predecessors, Al Qaeda brought us the tragic terrorist attacks of 9/11.

As we all know, these were the most devastating choreographed terrorist attacks the world has ever known; costing the lives of three thousand innocent bystanders, many of whom were the zenith of the financial world and others who representing New York's finest First Responders. Beyond the immediate casualties, the carnage destroyed countless lives, tore apart families and caused almost irreparable damage to the American psyche.

The 9/11 events were followed by a string of other heinous acts of terror around the world. This was reciprocated in kind with our own military campaign and the invasion of Afghanistan; approximately two decades after we helped the ancestors of this terrorist militia fight the Soviets.

We are still waging the war in Afghanistan today, over sixteen years later. Many actually believe this was the start of the 27-year World War III the west would wage against the Anti-Christ which Michel de Nostradame (known to most as "Nostradamus") predicted all the way back in the mid-sixteenth century.

As if this wasn't bad enough of a boomerang, it was not the end of it. From Al Qaeda, a more violent and

extreme (yes, apparently that was possible) splinter
group emerged. It was founded by Abu Musab al-
Zarqawi, operated under the helm of Abu Musab al-
Zarqawi and called ISIS ("Islamic State of Iraq and
Syria"), ISIL ("Islamic State of Iraq and the Levant"),
IS ("Islamic State") or by it's Arabic acronym, Daesh.

Capturing world attention and gaining prominence
when, amidst the chaos that reigned in Syria since it's
civil war commenced during the Arab Spring of 2011
(and is still on-going at present- December, 2017)) as
well as Iraq's weak and unstable government installed
following the toppling of one Saddam Hussein (nope,
no "Weapons of Mass Destruction" were ever found-
that was quite the boo boo, mais non...?), it
established a modern-day Caliphate, or Islamic State
(because that's precisely what the world needed) in
eastern Iraq and "The Levant" (or, "Syria" for white
people).

By the way, a "Caliphate", is a devout Muslim state
led by an Islamic steward known as a "Caliph"; a
successor to the Islamic prophet Muhammad.

In the Syrian campaign, Bashar Assad used chemical
warfare to annihilate villages indiscriminately. The
U.S. "drew a line in the sand" promising sever
repercussions should that ever occur. President
Barack Obama did nothing. By contrast, just a few
years before, though no WMD's were ever found in
Iraq, the U.S. and its allies (with the help of

contracted private mercenaries and logistics companies which enjoyed a somewhat incestuous relationship with many of the top politicians of the day…) waged a massive war (then parceled out that nation's re-building to the likes of Halliburton, Carlyle and such…) resulting in a regime change which ousted Saddam Hussein. Ironic how that all pans out, isn't it…?

As of the end of 2017, the Caliphate is crumbling and ISIS suffered tremendous set-backs, but just today (the first day of December, 2017), I read about the next incarnation of ISIS; lone wolf attacks, a return to guerrilla warfare and such… in both The Washington Post and The New York Times. Who knows what the future holds, but going back to Nostradamus, we still have over a decade of bickering to persevere. Good luck everyone!

To further illustrate how capable we are of alignment with unsavory "partners" (even concurrently on multiple fronts), it is worth mentioning General Manuel Noureiga of Panama and the Sandinistas from Nicaragua (remember the "Iran-Contra", aka "Irangate", aka "Contragate" scandal…?); both were entanglements which lead to equally disastrous catastrophes.

The abuse of power and the delusions of grandeur it is intrinsically tied to has many faces. I am, once again, VERY sorry for the diversion, but it is important to touch on these things and, at least, put them out there, even as a quick recap as was done here, because *"If we do not learn from our history, we are destined to repeat it."*

Actually, you should watch Oliver Stone's prolific historical documentary series, "The Untold History of the United States"- Yes, it too can be found, like most of life's answers, on Netflix.

5 CONSIDERATIONS AND SUGGESTIONS FOR PERSONAL GROWTH

Needless to say at this point, but a lot of the ideas, suggestions and concepts belonging in this section have already been covered insofar as what we say, how we act or who we ultimately present ourselves as, but, wait! There's just a bit more...

We've covered our very basic needs and those principles of managing and prioritizing our resources, namely time, and how we should conduct ourselves.

Here, we'll examine areas often so often overlooked in our lives today, but so very essential for our wellbeing- A sense of balance, our trust factor and level of happiness. Others are much simpler, quite ridiculous to mention actually, but also often not addressed, such as; reading, a hobby, traveling and the like.

Originating with our basic needs, but embellishing and augmenting them significantly as well as categorizing the different levels of priority they hold, Abraham Maslow, in his 1943 paper "A Theory of Human Motivation" in the periodical Psychological Review presented "Maslow's Hierarchy of Needs". They include the following levels in sequential order of importance and the needs each stage addresses:

Physiological- Breathing, food, water, sex, sleep, homeostasis and excretion.

Safety- Security of body, of employment, of resources, of morality, of family, of health and of property.

Love/Belonging- Friendship, family and sexual intimacy.

Esteem- Self-esteem, confidence, achievement and respect of and by others.

Self-Actualization- Morality, creativity, spontaneity, problem solving, lack of prejudice and acceptance of facts.

Maslow subsequently extended the above to include his observations of humans' innate curiosity.

Others take a different approach, dividing our needs and desires to personal and public; introvert and extrovert, or; intrinsic and external. Whatever you label these as, there is a clear line between what our needs are and that which we aspire to attain, on a personal level versus the public eye.

Whichever delineation is used, and while the importance and amount of each differs from one person to another, intrinsically, we all need to have nourishing close relationships with friends, relatives and companions, have a desire to help our fellow man and so forth. Externally, or in the public eye as it were, we all seek a positive public image/ persona and status that are revered and held in a high regard by our colleagues, peers and even strangers.

All of these lead to one ultimate goal- Being happy. Although it is one of our basic and most primal feelings, surprisingly, the study of happiness is relatively new. In the 1990's a class in "Positive Psychology" was first offered at Harvard. The response was immediate and overwhelming- It drew the student body's attention and became an extremely popular class with a long waiting list instantaneously.

I reckon, just like the topic of sex, arriving at the annals of education about three decades prior, people were also interested in this subject that was equally overlooked by a millennia of curriculum in university studies.

In the largely infant filed of positive psychology, it is assumed that happiness is 50% genetic (our "base" or "starting point"), 10% circumstantial (income, where & how you live, social status, etc.) and 40% intentional activity (actions you choose; freewill). The subject is examined thoroughly and globally in the documentary "Happy", directed by Roko Belic (Yes, on Netflix as well…).

Happiness releases dopamine. It brings us pleasure; both physical and mental. It leads to a healthier lifestyle, increased productivity, potentially leading to a better career, thus maximizing your professional life and getting you closer to realizing your full potential and attaining your goals. By the way, the two biggest contributors to one's happiness level are close family and friends.

As we wrote at the onset of our relationship dozens of pages ago, being fulfilled and happy also manifests and extends itself to others. You'll be a pleasure to be around, more (willing to assist and) helpful to others, project a more positive attitude, words and actions towards life. As noted, we will also be more apt to gravitate towards and surround ourselves with like-minded individuals who (hopefully) are "evolved and elevated" or those with "high vibrational frequency" who will make you more likely to practice a healthy & fulfilling lifestyle, thus, more apt to attain success, love, harmony, solace and fulfillment. In essence, attract & invite happy, positive people into our lives. Simply put, this is the law of positive attraction.

Consistently propagating this effect will increase it in an exponential manner that, if successful, will ultimately make a substantial difference in this becoming a better world for us all.

The world's last independent Buddhist monarchy, Bhutan, actually adopted this exponential utilitarian effect on its citizenry by opting to measure the country's quality of life in terms of it's Gross National Happiness per person as opposed to the more conventional Gross Domestic Product output per person.

Closer to home, the esteemed talk-show radio host and founder of the indispensable Prager U, Dennis Prager, dedicates an hour a week to the subject in his weekly "Happiness Hour".

At the heart of their constitution, one finds terms such as, "humility" and "compassion". Quite alien to declarations of this sort which are based the notions brought forth in the intellectual and scientific movement of 18th century Europe known as The Age of Enlightenment. Back then, humanity was just beginning to understand the notions of individual liberties and inherent rights with the promise of

"*Liberté, égalité, fraternité*"; the national motto of the Third Republic of France (and it's distant colony, Haiti), which assured "*liberty, equality, fraternity*" is bestowed upon all it's citizenry.

Quite a leap, especially considering the short period of time between the two theories making their way into the national psyche as well as the economic disparity between the two- Bhutan, clearly a third world economy while France is in the "Group of 7" which is comprised of the world's seven leading economies. Further proof that, at least where enlightenment and happiness are concerned where money isn't everything...

The people of Bhutan are actually ranked among the happiest on earth despite their very low per capita income. Relative to France as compared above, it is just under one fifth- Yes, less than 20%.

A recent poll trying to seek a correlation between happiness and income surprised many people. There was a tremendous rise in the level of happiness between zero income and the level of basic sustenance (in this study, it was $70K annually per household, but the figure is a dynamic one as it is supposed to signify a financial benchmark defining "basic sustenance" which of course varies from time to time, place to place and person to person).

Regardless, whatever that figure is, between it and an annual income of, say, a million dollars, the increase in the level of happiness is negligible. By the way, the million dollar figure is also arbitrary; there is virtually nil difference moving it to ten million, one hundred million, a billion dollars a year; whatever...

Insofar as money is concerned, the overwhelming increase in the level of happiness it brings people, is essentially only apparent and matters between being destitute and being able to take care of our own and our family's basic necessities. If we leave the definition of those "basic necessities" to the person being questioned, there is absolutely no correlation between income and happiness levels beyond that point at all...

Unrelated to the above, but a reflection on happiness of a different kind, the astute Oscar Wilde cleverly said: "*Some (people) cause happiness wherever they go; others, whenever they go.*"

What is correlated with happiness is in fact another often overlooked trait in a society, it's trust factor. Esteban-Ortiz Ospina and Max Roser of the non-profit organization "Our World in Data" point out that, at one extreme, there are countries with a high trust factor. In a recent study called the World Value Survey, these include the Scandinavian nations of

Norway (the leader by far), Sweden and Finland as well as Switzerland where over 60% of respondents said they think people can be trusted. On the other extreme, countries such as the Philippines, Zimbabwe, Ghana, Colombia, Ecuador, Brazil and Romania are at the other end with less than 10% trust. Although not exactly uniform, but the level of "trust" in people overall is about the same when questioned about their fellow citizens, the police or their government.

A few glaring differences are that Germany is about double the level of it's very similar socioeconomic European neighbor, France, and that Hong Kong, Vietnam and China rank remarkably high compared to their Asian counterpart (yes, even Japan).

The United States is ranked quite high compared to the OECD countries' average (24% versus 38%), but a recent Pew Research Center survey found the U.S. at a historically low level in terms of people's trust in government; down 40% in just a few decades. In fact, people trust each other in the U.S. much more than either the government or the police.

Not surprisingly, the top ranked nations have relatively small populations and are extremely wealthy. Beyond that, with very few exceptions, they also enjoy low poverty rates and crime levels (the disparity grows significantly in terms of violent crimes) and represent the highest standard of living, quality of life and happiness quotient on our planet.

Back to the most important person in this relationship between us- YOU.

Her endless complaints and criticisms aside, one life lesson my mom gave me which I hold dear to my heart is that, even in airplanes, when the flight attendant reviews the protocol to follow in the event of an emergency, he/she always underscore the importance of putting the life vest on your own body first, then attending to others. Yes, even before your children.

You see, if you are not well, you ain't gonna be much good for your kids, or your parents, grandparents, or your husband or wife, or girlfriend or boyfriend nor anyone for that matter.

Several years ago, I read an article that disturbed me. It was well before the current opiate epidemic, but it's focus was on one of the fastest growing segments of society using methamphetamines, or stimulants. The article discussed single mothers who used the narcotic to be able to accomplish all they needed to do in life.

The sleepless nights, the long hours at work (at times, more than one job) the cooking, cleaning, laundry, shopping, homework with the kids, their extracurricular activities, after-school programs, tutors, doctors, dentists and orthodontists, the back to school nights, PTA, teacher-parent conferences, school shows, holiday performances, homecoming, dances, formals and the prom and, no- IT NEVER ENDS. The stress is never ending and the pressure just builds and mounts from day to day. That truly disturbed me, so, if you are a single mom or dad, these next pages are especially relevant and important for you.

Whether single or married, parents are those people that are responsible for the seeds of our future and our collective wellbeing. They are the guardians of the hope for mankind. So PLEASE do not stop reading now.

Just as the example above noted; the one with the airplane in case of an emergency… And just as I wrote regarding this relationship, take care of Number One first- YOU.

I know there isn't time, and I know you have no money, and I know you don't have the energy, but PLEASE, for the sake of those who depend on you- Your children, your mate, your parents, your grandparents, your extended family, your close friends, your colleagues, your employees, your co-workers, your students, your patients, your clients, whomever… Try your very best to take care of yourself. Just read and implement whatever you can, you want or that which you feel may be beneficial for you as a person and make your life just a little bit better.

Life is a number's game- Statistics and probabilities and so forth. So, adopt and employ a few good habits, sleep an hour more, eat a little better, exercise just a few minutes every day, take the stairs instead of the elevator (where applicable) or instead of the escalator, read from time to time, take a relaxing bath, get a massage or, the ever so trite, take a walk on the beach, watch the sunset and smell the flowers… Believe it or not, all of these do make a difference and, with several components combined, the aggregate effect will enhance the quality of your life. In turn, this will make you better equipped and a better person to accomplish all that you need to as best as you can.

Try to use people's experience as a guide when making decisions or choices. We covered a lot of turf, with a lot more coming. It would behoove you and be beneficial for you to extract whichever ideas or suggestions you believe apply to you and can improve your life in one way or another. Remember the saying *"If I only knew then what I know now"*…? That is the precise reason you are reading this book. Extracting and practicing that which makes sense for you, will inevitably save you endless aggravation, tons of money and time, which is so very precious; and so very finite.

Just like Stuart Smalley did on "Saturday Night Live", give yourself daily affirmations (even if it sounds pointless and/or stupid). As we've covered ad nauseam, write- Your ideas and your goals; then make sure you're on track (if you are not, get yourself back on track). Manage your time constantly, prioritize, evaluate value (regardless if it's a friend, the importance of a chore or the price of something you desire), understand opportunity cost and what you have given up, or sacrificed, in lieu of attaining or obtaining something else. Remember, everything has a price and our resources are both scarce and finite.

Be careful and mindful of whom you surround yourself with and who you let in. For all the many and important reasons outlined before; and because they truly are an extension of who you are and a reflection of your own image by others. Yes- Your friends and relatives do affect how outsiders regard you.

Never stop observing, questioning, investigating, challenging, researching, examining, learning and studying. Remain curious and you'll always be relevant. In terms of learning, try to read more in general. First, regardless of what it is, reading (and speaking foreign tongues) are two of the only known "exercises" which prevent, or at least delay, diseases associated with the cognitive decline due to aging.

In a similar vein, if you run across something you are interested in, like or wish to learn about, take a minute and Shazam that song, Wikipedia that person, place or thing, look up that word or phrase in a dictionary or thesaurus. Of course you can just google these (can you believe that's a damn verb already!).

Learn a new language, even though it is truly an exercise in futility given today's technology. As we already know, it'll help prevent, or at least delay, cognitive deterioration-related diseases and, as my father so rightfully pointed out, every language you learn, "...it's as if you're another person". Not that I'm advocating complicating this already complex world with more multiple personalities and schizophrenia cases, but the man has a point.

Learn about yourself too- Spend a few dollars and find out what makes you, well, you... through 23andme or Ancestry. It might shed some light on a few habits, neurosis or predispositions you might have and, by unveiling your roots, maybe bring about a sense of belonging and identity.

So, read for leisure, for the purpose of expanding your knowledge base related to your career, and to quell information you are seeking about those things you wish to explore, investigate and learn about. Just read… It'll educate you, add to your intelligence AND keep you healthy.

Dr. Charles William Eliot compiled and edited "The Harvard Universal Classics" books, originally known as, "Dr. Eliot's Five Foot Shelf". It consisted of a 51-volume anthology of classic works with each volume consisting of 400-450 pages. When placed upright next to each other, as books should be, measure (surprise, surprise) five feet. The notion was that the elements of a liberal education could be obtained by reading just 15 minutes each day.

This brilliant, yet quite minimal, intellectual "overview" of humanity utilizing and exploring every social and liberal arts discipline. A similar approach to the one originally conceived just about a millennia ago at the Hohenburg Abbey in Alsace, France (a gorgeous city by a lake) by the Herrad of Landsberg-The medieval manuscript, Hortus Deliciarum, "… encompassing those universal principles which are the condition of the possibility of the existence of anything and everything".

Basically, if everyone universally reads and comprehends five feet of books, we're good to go!

For this; and much else on the following pages, you'll need to make sure you have some "me" time. I know it's virtually impossible- The two spawns of Lucifer who are my children (this is obviously said in complete jest, or "LOL" as it is now known) don't let me shower in peace, they don't even "allow" private toilet time. Worse than Warden Drumgoole of "Lock Up", I swear. And any attempt at correcting that very narcissistic and unacceptable behavior, or to "negotiate" my well-deserved (perhaps even my unalienable right to...) personal time/space, are usually in vain. All of that being true, still get a few moments for yourself and make it a rule for the others. You must do this for your sanity, to clear your mind a bit and re-charge before returning to the battlefield that is life.

There's a song from the old country that translates into "*A man, within himself he lives*". While not the best sounding proverb when translated, it essentially means we live within ourselves- Our consciousness, ethics, morals, the mind within our brain that provokes thought & spurs our imagination culminating in our ideas, goals and aspirations. With today's VR and AR capabilities, these words have never been more true.

This all leads us to the concept "Minimalism". We actually need very to survive, even to thrive. You can keep & contain all that you really need within a hand's reach; by your bedside or your desk at the office. Unloading unnecessary baggage, in the form of old girl or boyfriends, toxic people, unnecessary objects; whether rendered useless by innovation, your current state of life, or an article of clothing's outdated style; or you "growing" out of a particular size.

EVERYTHING, regardless if it's a person or an object, everything depletes resources- Time, attention, thought, etc. An old urn you hate still takes up space and still needs to get dusted. An old flame still occupies your mind and prevents you from making the right choice or from having a healthy relationship. And so forth…

Think of the amount of time, energy, money and other resources you would save if you eliminated only a few undesirable elements from your life. Imagine how much more open minded, at peace, fresher, more productive and effective you would be if you only focused on what matters and filtered out the rest…?

We know we don't have enough time, enough money, nor enough energy to do all that we set out to achieve. As such, as benign as it may appear, just like with a complex machine, code or production process (as we have reviewed above with running cities or big operations smoothly, or making films, or anything for that matter…), *"it's the small things that enable the big things to happen."*

As such, seemingly stupid habits, like putting everything in it's place, can and do add up in aggregate; and the more of these you do, the bigger the benefit at the end. Just as with the example cited here, how many hours, or days, will you save over a lifetime if you didn't need to look for shit that was lost; or waste your time cleaning up after your kids because they just leave their toys, games, art and craft supplies, homework or clothing anywhere they feel like...

It is no wonder therefore that all religions teach the doctrines of minimalism. Other than a handful of televangelists (of past and present) and a few unscrupulous scoundrels posing as pious religious leaders (of ALL strains), every religious figure- From the Shaolin Buddhist monk, to the missionary priest somewhere in Africa, Zoroaster the prophet, the Enlightened Siddhartha or Mother Teresa doing miracles and saving lives all the way in Kolkata (formerly, Calcutta) all exalts the virtues and benefits of minimalism.

The merits of minimalism are embodied in virtually every culture, family and commercial enterprise. From the aspects of frugality to status and even those pertaining to reward or financial compensation, humility and minimalism do offer any person a clearer perspective, a slate devoid of noise, an open mind and

resources pointed & dedicated to wherever you want
them focused at and sacrificed for.

Not to beat a dead horse, but with the current virtual
and augmented reality, who gives a shit how lavish or
palatial your mansion is. These "new realm" are
game-changers not just for playing "pretend" or video
games, but for flight, exercise, surgery, combat
training, among other simulation applications; even
traveling from an entirely new perspective.

When my brother and I grew older and started
driving, my father would wake up early on weekend
mornings and take all of our cars to the car wash and
get them filled up with gas. This was not only a
beautifully (recurring) gesture showing his love for us,
but also saving us from doing so, hence a lot of time.

While trends vary, depending largely on the size of
any specific city, whether people live at it's nexus or
only on it's outskirts (or suburbs) and, of course, the
availability, reliability and dependability of it's public
transportation system/s, the average American
worker commutes for 45 minutes and spends $12
each day on their roundtrip commute. This is
obviously significantly worse in the large urban
employment Meccas of New York (where the average
roundtrip commute is 73 min, with 44% of residents
commuting for over an hour) or in Los Angeles
(where there is little remedy in the form of public

transport, hence L.A. boasts the biggest cost, at $16 per day). Other cities that fall in this category include San Francisco, Washington DC, Trenton, Boston, Atlanta, Chicago, Seattle and Houston. In all of these, the national average of 200 hours (that's FIVE work weeks) and a $2,600 annual cost are of course grossly understated.

Given the above, plan and put this time to good use- Rest, read the news or answer emails if you're in public transport and, if traveling in your own vehicle, schedule calls for that time or dictate correspondence. Whatever it is, don't let the time go to waste.

When lamenting on what we can do individually to affect change in the larger scheme of things, it is worth noting that our current carpool rate is 1.1 (drivers per car); virtually nil. If that was increased to just 1.6 drivers per car, all of our regular (those not resulting from accidents or roadwork) traffic jams would cease to exist.

Speaking of time, just to illustrate how our race is not all that sophisticated, the concept of exact time in human civilization (as opposed to saying "I'll see you around noon" or "... at lunchtime") is less than 200 years old. Yes, it was only with the spread of steam-powered railway trains that humans needed to adopt the concept of precise time.

First published in 2008 "The Blue Zone- Lessons for Living Longer from the People who've Lived the Longest" a book by Dan Buettner and Ed Dienar, which has, over the past decade, transformed into an ecosystem of life improving products as well as a full-fledged project adopting the diets, rituals, environments and other lifestyle characteristics of societies known for longevity. In one of these regions, the Greek island of Ikaria in the Mediterranean, also known as "The island where people forget to die", the Centenarians say that one of the factors allowing them to enjoy the longevity they do is attributed to the lack of rushing and haste that virtually defines modern lives everywhere else. Being devoid of a strict schedule and the pressure of constant time-sensitive commitments every day, enables the people to live their lives more naturally, at their own pace, at ease and in peace. They do not achieve any less; they just do things according to their schedule; NOT the other way around. Just sayin'...

There is an old Italian adage- *"Chi va piano, va sano e va lontano"* loosely translated, it means *"He who walks slow, walks long and far"*. The island of Ikaria proves these words are true. So, while you should definitely be assertive, confident and driven, also remember to be patient- Life isn't a one hundred-yard dash; it is most definitely a marathon.

We humans respond well to rewards. Just recall the Russian physiologist Ivan Petrovich Pavlov. His work involved research in temperament, involuntary reflex actions, but he is most remembered for his theory on classical conditioning. Simply put, in an experiment, Pavlov rang a bell and fed some dogs. In time, the canines were conditioned to associate the ringing bell with receiving food. At one time, the bell rang, but no food was placed for the dogs; guess what, they salivated in anticipation of being fed. Exactly the same with our species.

Keeping that in mind, remember to reward yourself and those around you. Whether it's ice cream, a drive along the beach, watching your favorite show, setting yourself a goal to accomplish, then rewarding yourself for attaining it, is a good practice. Also, do not be afraid to pamper yourself from time to time- Getting a massage, your nails done, having a drink (or ten); just be mature about it and be responsible. The same obviously applies to your spouse or mate, children, employees and so forth.

The first and easiest reward one can give it expressing gratitude or acknowledgement to another. Just like a compliments, a few genuine words can go a long way; for both the recipient and the one bestowing the kindness.

In 2004, I was blessed to be able to attend the music and arts "Burning Man" festival in Black Rock City. First, I should note that, if at all possible, this is one adventure I highly and wholeheartedly recommend

you experience at least once in your life. Despite the
reputation of "sex, drugs and electronic music" (not
that there's anything wrong with that...), nor the fact
that the event has been tremendously
"commercialized" as the years pass, this gathering in
which a fully operational city is built, then demolished
within a few weeks without leaving a trace, each
group of people is completely self-sustained (at least
they're supposed to be) and trade is based strictly on a
barter economy, also offers a lot in terms of personal
growth, moral elevation, mindfulness and, if your
mind is open, exposure to interesting people, eye-
opening ideas and thought provoking concepts
almost unique to this spiritual expedition.

You get the point... At any rate, the story I was
attempting to tell is one about acknowledgement. As
a result of the barter society, each person takes a role
upon themselves, or a service they perform, in order
to offer that in exchange for other goods & services.
So I lead meditation sessions, you make juice
smoothies, she DJ's, he makes pizzas and so forth.

Well, I met a genius on two levels- The guy that gave
out acknowledgements. Not only was this genius
because there was no tangible cost for his vocation-
No raw materials, no supplies needed nor any
equipment. That said, it was a transformative
experience in many way. We made small talk, he
explained what he does, then asked me what is it in

my life that I did, was proud of, yet never received any gratitude or acknowledgement for.

I told him about my stepson of sorts. He's not legally my stepson- I dated his mom from when he was 7 until the age of 13. After we broke up, she moved away and he went to live with his dad, also far away. He and I only became closer with time, establishing our own very, peculiar perhaps, but extremely strong bond. As I was the only "adult" left where his entire social life was based following the break up, we spent a lot of weekends together, and grew even closer. This was one relationship that took a lot of time and effort for which I had no knowledge or any guidance for. That was what I was seeking acknowledgement for and, after a few moments speaking about the subject, the acknowledgement I received from a total stranger was one of the most personal and sentimental moments of life to this very day.

Today, almost 15 years later, that kid is in his early 30's, has been living in Shanghai for the past decade (he is Chinese/Vietnamese/American), is doing tremendously well both professionally and socially and is, as he always has been, a positive influence & contributing member of society.

He teaches young children how to overcome their fear of public speaking, trains executives to better deliver their intended message and teaches diplomats how to bridge cultural divides. I'm serious- NO shit.

Needless to say, I could not be more proud of his achievements and what he has become.

Happiness releases dopamine as noted. It therefore no wonder that laughter stimulates the release of other feel-good substances, including endorphins, such as the opiate OxyContin. These opiates are sedative narcotics capable of relieving pain and unleashes growth hormones which promote growth, metabolism and overall better health. By the way, the opiate epidemic will be discussed later; in a much different light of course.

So we need to smile and laugh more. One proven way to achieve that is getting a pet. Pets are now legally recognized as "emotional support" mechanisms for the ailing and the elderly. They promote immunity, a longer life, reduce stress and anxiety while providing companionship to many forgotten souls who most need the leaping welcome of a pet when they arrive at home and to feel their warmth as they recline or sit by you vying for love and attention.

As clearly established, and since we are (for the most part...) social animals, we need companionship-Family, friends and pets. In terms of friends, most people actually have very few true friends; usually a handful. These are not "acquaintances", but true close friends. Of these, it is highly recommended to have ONE genuine confidant, preferably non-related. This of course is needed BOTH for seeking advice or just to vent (or, conversely, to learn how to listen...).

When you are sure of a specific stance, decision or course of action that needs to take place, or if the discussion revolves your area of expertise or field of interest, you should, actually must, insist on your position. If the right answer, choice or path is absolutely clear and evident to you, be assertive, even stubborn, in defending that conclusion, point of view or course of action. As John Wick had inked in Latin across his shoulders; "*Fortis Fortuna Adiuvat*" (or, "*Fortune Favors the Bold*").

To underline yet again the importance of having a determined attitude and an adamant, relentless pursuit of a goal, we return to Ayn Rand. Ms. Rand's first two novels were a miserable failure prior to the arrival of her acclaimed novel, "The Fountainhead", ten full years later which brought her much fame when first published in 1943.

Beyond the unfolding of her own reality recounted above, the protagonist of her novel, "The Fountainhead", is Howard Roark- A brilliant young architect who, like the author herself, despite the reviews, the scrutiny, the envy and the scorn, stood his ground and never succumbed. Just as prescribed above.

The courtroom speech of the book's film adaptation, delivered in outstanding form by the renowned actor, Gary Cooper in the role of Howard Roark, which explains the reasoning of the above is indispensable viewing (as is the entire film). In his speech, Mr. Roark explains what we covered several pages ago, whilst covering brainstorming- That every inventor or great thinker bringing forth a new idea or concept was ridiculed, ostracized or branded as a lunatic at best; and burned at the stake at worst.

In the art world, it is a well known fact that, almost universally, art appreciates in value once it's creator has passed away. This of course is partially dependent on the popularity of the artist in question at any given time. Other than that variable dynamic, of course a deceased artist cannot create more inventory, hence the supply is finite, though, in some cases, like that of the Pablo Picasso, who left a multi-billion dollar cache of some 45,000 works, that is hardly an issue...

Another major factor attributing to the rising price of these artworks upon or after an artist's death; or late in their lives, is that, in many cases, it was only late in life (or after their death), that their work garner the respect, nor even receive acceptance, by the art world; a very finicky bunch many times directed by a just handful of art arbiters.

Such was the fate of many of the greatest artists of all time, in more contemporary times (as getting "discovered" during the Renaissance may have proven to be a bit harder than today...), they include the following (VERY minimal) gifted masters: Amedeo Clemente Modigliani, Vincent van Gough, Mary Delany, Paul Cézanne and my very favorite (and more recent) such story; Carmen Herrera who, at the tender age of 101 (while living in Manhattan, mind you...) finally received the respect the world should have afforded her many decades ago. At the end of 2016, she got to show her work in a major solo museum exhibition at the Whitney Museum of American Art, "Carmen Herrera: Lines of Sight", prominent gallery presence and a biographical documentary feature entitled "The 100 Years Show, Starring Carmen Herrera" (yup, on Netflix as well). Perseverance and persistence take a whole new meaning when reading stories such as these.

In most cases, talent rises to the surface, just as the truth is ultimately uncovered; both are things we would equally like to believe as humans conditioned to seek, almost "expect", a "happy ending" where justice prevails. The above illustrates the payoff for the undying human spirit. Opposite of these stories about talent being discovered and rewarded, justice of course also pertains to the redemption we seek from those who have wronged others, just as the vile sexual predators discussed earlier- Bringing them to justice and making them pay for their crimes.

I have a friend whose siblings are at least twenty years his senior, he was clearly not a planned pregnancy; and his parents didn't exactly take measures to disguise that fact... To augment that wonderful contribution to his confidence, his folks were Holocaust survivors which, in most cases, (and understandably so) meant they harbored some dark demons deep in their psyche which exposed themselves from time to time. To add even more, they passed when he was relatively young; his father following eight years in a state of comatose. And, to top it all off, a very close relative who was supposed to protect him wound up jacking him in business rather significantly; and guess which one of them was actually doing most of the work...?

That man immigrated to the U.S. Needless to say, with no papers, a profession, money nor even proper English. All he came with was a dream, unbridled resilience and, despite the emotional toll of his baggage, a positive outlook on life and optimism like nothing I have ever witnessed; before or since...

"Smile unto the world and the world...", yeah right... but this guy persevered and pursued and remained on course and would not relent. Today he is happily married for almost 20 years, has two beautiful, intelligent and healthy girls, not to mention a thriving construction business- The life every man should aspire to attain AND maintain.

Conversely, *"Face your demons"*- In order to defeat, surpass and eradicate your worst fears and nightmares, you must face them. Similar in outcome to the instinctive *"fight or flight"* mechanism, the result will determine if your fears haunt and consume you or whether you overcome and lay them to waste, thereby freeing so much to point and focus on more fruitful endeavors.

Precisely as you should be adamant, steadfast, even stubborn, when you are sure of something; if you are unsure or just don't know, it is equally imperative you admit as much and make that known too. There is no shame whatsoever in admitting something is outside the scope of your knowledge (or interest, or expertise). In fact, doing the opposite, as so many people do for the sake of their own vanity or to feed their egos (or look good in front of their peers), is not only short-sided, but wrong and, depending on the circumstance or importance of the decision on the agenda, could be detrimental to any business, family or your life.

On a related note, engaging in what the Hebrews referred to as *"lashon hara"*- sometimes confused with defamation, the real Halakhic ("Halacha" is the collective body of Jewish laws derived from the Torah, or Old Testament) definition of this term is the use of true facts for a wrongful purpose, rather than falsehood. It is detraction- Saying something

true, but negative, about a person that is not seriously
intended to correct or improve a negative situation.

In short, try to not judge others, be accepting and
open-minded (despite your neurosis, biases and
prejudices, as noted above). In essence, "*Live and let
live*".

Bringing this idea to some examples in our lives, in
politics, it is said, "*you cannot insult someone then ask for
their vote*". By the same token, you cannot tell an
employee how stupid they are and that, next time,
they better follow your lead. Remember, even a
broken clock is right twice a day.

Also, when someone sends you a disparaging text, as
my mom often does for no reason (generally, it is for
one reason- because she makes certain assumptions
she believes in wholeheartedly with no rhyme or
reason whatsoever), then asks why I am so upset all
the time; and that I really need to take care of my
anger management issues when, in fact, I was
absolutely fine; happy, positive and motivated just
moments before receiving her venomous words…

This approach which unfortunately is used more
often and in more facets of our life we'd even care to
admit leads only to bad results- Loss of loyalty,
appreciation, interest or respect, discourse, even

mutiny. Whatever the consequence is, it will be negative- The only variable is to what extent... So, think before you write or say anything and try not to take this road whenever possible. For example (and sheerly by experience unfortunately...), if I must write a negative letter or email for whatever reason, I write it, then sleep on it before sending out to make sure I still want to send it and ascertain I do not look ridiculous or put myself in harm's way by having an emotional or knee-jerk reaction to something someone said or wrote. As the adage goes, *"it is easier to get honey with honey. If you use vinegar, that it most likely what you'll get in return"*...

Another common practice you should let go of is putting people down without a proper cause or for no reason. Contrary to popular belief (especially of individuals with low self esteem, self worth or those driven by ego), this vile practice does not make you more attractive, anymore "right", "smarter", "bigger" or "better". And, again, it's a pointless waste of time and resources.

An extension of the above is to try and minimize criticizing or passing judgement. That said, if it is absolutely necessary, warranted and needed, do so with sincerity, try not to be demeaning or condescending, and do so in privacy to avoid unnecessary public humiliation (unless that is your intent, of course...).

In a similar vein, don't talk under your breath or as you walk away. If you have something to say, say it with clarity conviction and purpose. Only then do your words truly matter, are taken seriously and can have the full desired effect.

On the opposite end, always keep this in mind; *"Just because you're offended does not mean you are right"* and don't stress when put under duress or threatened because *"A dog that barks seldom bites"*. The ones you must be leery of are the quiet ones or "the strong silent types". Just like correlation I can attest to personally between women and adventurous sex; the quiet ones are usually the freaky (and much more fun) partners. No, I am not being sexist; this is true for men and women alike.

You should try to minimize your judgment and criticism of others' words and/or actions, especially as it pertains to life or relationship critique/"assessment" you hand out.

As we know too well, *"the worst VICE is adVICE"*- Even if your intentions are pure, you cannot fully know one's emotional baggage or fully comprehend their childhood or surroundings, nor understand the demons that lurk within which all contributed to the molding of any person and culminated in a final product which is who they are today, thus leading them in a specific direction or to make certain choices. Needless to say, if your best friend (you juveniles refer to them by the acronym "BFF", I believe), is actively seeking advice, by all means, give him/her your two cents, but no more than two... That said, don't make the mistake of giving advice when a friend is only seeking a shoulder to cry on or an ear to vent to...

The same is true with relationship advice to others-No one knows the history, has transparent access to both sides of the relationship, nor knowledge of what goes on behind closed doors or in the bed, so, unless you best buddy is dating a bi-polar psychopath and you must alert his attention to that fact in order to save his life, try to keep your comments to yourself.

As noted, people should make their own choices and choose their own path. Your job is to help them obtain the tools and the foundation needed to make the right choices, then mentor and support them along the way.

Imagine the following scenario. You have a stock tip. You want to share it with a good friend who's playing the market. Why...? If he makes a killing, he'll do his utmost and whatever he can to try and hide it from you. If he loses, in his eyes, you'll be the liable culprit and guilty of misguiding or misinforming him. It's a classic "Catch 22" situation-Damned if you do and damned if you don't; i.e., NO WAY OUT...

Just as when your lover, girlfriend or wife asks: "Do I
look fat in these jeans…?". There is no right answer
to that question my friend, trust me.

Side note: The phrase "Catch 22" was coined in the
1961 eponymous dark satiric novel by Joseph Heller,
adapted to film in 1970 and starring an ensemble cast,
which included; Orson Welles, Alan Arkin, Art
Garfunkel, Anthony Perkins, Jon Voight, Martin
Balsam, Martin Sheen, Paula Prentiss, Buck Henry,
Richard Benjamin, Jack Gilford and Bob Newhart.
WOW!!! Indeed.

Another time-wasting diversion to avoid is dwelling
on your past. To succeed in the future, you must let
go of the past. Come to terms with it, resolve it;
whatever it takes. Let go of that bad break-up,
someone close that has passed, the kids leaving the
nest for college, or what could have been or should
have been.

As tough as it may be, try to reminisce on good
memories, adapt as best as possible to the new
circumstances, focus on your goal, look forward to
the future and the promise it holds. That's all we can
do Holmes.

As has been covered ad nauseam, since time, money, energy and essentially all resources are finite and scarce, I cannot stress enough how important it is to conserve your mojo and other resources so they can be expended on more worthwhile endeavors (this, naturally, is linked to the concept "opportunity cost", scheduling and, of course, prioritizing; all of which we have already discussed in great detail).

All religions prescribe charity and benevolence. To be exact, most put the figure at ten percent of your earnings- Christians, Muslims and Jews alike (don't even get me started with Buddhists or Hindus, you'll have nothing left...). However you phrase it- Give to charity, give back to the community, pay it forward and so forth, donate BOTH some of your time and money (as they represent two very distinct forms of charity and present the donor with entirely different rewards).

When donating money, doing so anonymously or eponymously are VERY different as well. For example, just donating a bunch of cash to your favorite cause and receiving no credit for it, nor any requirements or expectations of acknowledgement from the recipient versus getting a plaque, a brick, a bench, even a cancer research facility named after you or a loved one. Either way, giving is good, so GIVE- It's good for those who need it and it's good for your Karmic balance sheet.

Related to the discussion about wealth distribution (more appropriately, "concentration") a few pages ahead, the silver lining of the very extreme concentration of wealth and power in so few hands is that, for the time being, in more cases than not, the tenets of giving and charity are deeply ingrained in many of the most powerful and richest people on earth.

Notably, is the example and challenge set forth by the Bill & Melinda Gates Foundation whereby the mighty tycoons and today's Great Gatsby's can donate the overwhelming majority of their wealth to charitable organizations. This notion of giving is a milestone in the evolution of charity and should be applauded no less than Billy's other achievements, such as the BASIC program, initially brought to market in 1963, which he redesigned in 1975 to MITS ("micro instrumentation and telemetry systems") for $3,000. Founded in 2000, as of 2006, Warren Buffet gave the foundation an astronomical $31 billion to be added to its coffers of $30 billion at the time.

Following the top two spots taken by Bill & Melinda Gates and Warren Buffet, the list of notable givers to charity include the who's who of the apex from many spheres of life- The great industrialists, the shrewd financiers, savvy investors, brightest inventors and other masterminds from every walk of life. Topping off the top ten greatest philanthropists of all time (by dollar amount donated directly, NOT what their foundations are valued at today) are: Li Ka-shing, Andrew Carnegie, Chuck Feeney, George Soros, Prince Al-Walled bin Talal, Azim Premji, Phil Knight and Howard Hughes. I truly did want to include a list of those who give back so handsomely, but upon closer scrutiny and some research, it appears this would take up such significant space (and your time) I elected to only mention those listed herein.

Echoing the above sentiment, Andrew Carnegie noted: *"The man who dies rich thus dies disgraced..."*.

I know this is just about the last thing you'd be thinking of right now and probably the furthest thing from your mind, but entertain the thought for just a minute (depending who you are, this of course could equally be applicable to you or your children...) - A year of public service, of giving back, of donating something from the individual "you" to better the collective, "us".

Contrary to popular belief or common misperception, I don't necessarily mean the military, but a year of volunteer work. Help local law enforcement, volunteer with the fire department, paramedics, or the Veteran's Administration, Peace Corps, Merchant Marines, Civilian Conservation Corps do some missionary work in the third world, be a civil humanitarian helping the poor, ill, elderly or disabled members of society, or join an NGO ("Non-Governmental Organization") domestically or abroad to fight, assist, correct, serve, help or otherwise aid a cause that is close to your heart. Whatever it is- A year of social service.

I know you're laughing and I know this ain't happening, but, if it would, the benefits, to both the recipients AND the donors, would be monumental and this practice would right a lot of wrongs. Countries that instill social responsibility in their populace generally enjoy a more thriving nation of people who understand, communicate and stand by their fellow man, a society that is predominantly peaceful and empathetic. Most importantly, a community that is homogeneous in terms of its values and moral standards. That, my friends, is priceless.

As I very ardently stated at the onset of our relationship, one of the elemental driving forces of my life is *"... Give everything you do 110% and you'll elevate the ordinary to the extraordinary"*. Also as discussed, this holds true for absolutely EVERYTHING we do in life.

Related to this notion is, perhaps, one of my greatest joys (and I shit you NOT) - Introducing others to new experiences and exposing them to new things; in every realm of life. New experiences and things of many natures and a myriad manifestations- Culinary, travel, cultural, artistic, musical, sexual; whatever new event or occurrence that takes place and engages one or more of our senses fall into this very substantial and significant form of human interaction.

No, I'm not on shrooms and I seem to have misplaced those annoying tiny LSD stamps, so I'm not on that either (just kidding- never done it, but am very much looking forward to it...). To bring this idea home, just recall the first time you had sex and whether your partner was supportive, giving, understanding, romantic and so forth... A good & positive first lover could lead you to a life of bliss and orgasmic fortitude, whereas the opposite will most likely destroy any drive you have and kill your "sex future". Sad, but true. Capiche?

I get such a rush from witnessing people experience something for the first time that, I can now admit that I often go overboard. It's the whole "*fish out of water*" concept and experience (as illustrated so magically in the film "City Slickers" which you may recall provided you're an oldie, comme moi), the opening of the eyes (and mind) in amazement, the anticipation, the imagination, the revelation- This, for me at least, is the stuff that dreams are made of.

My 80 or so year-old aunt (I never knew her true age because, in true Mid East female form, she lied) came to visit a couple of decades ago. Back in the old country, she was addicted to the soap opera "The Young and the Restless" (this was the early 90's, mind you). I happened to be producing films in those years

and actually knew one of the male leads of the series.
My cousin and I planned a little rendezvous- She
brought my aunt; I brought the stud and we met at a
landmark restaurant on the beach in Malibu. You can
only imagine what an amazing experience this was for
her- At first blushing & coy, but, by the end of her
"date", she had photos with her & her man frolicking
about on the shores of the Pacific (yes, of course one
of those was the image she used for her holiday
greeting cards…).

Surely, you can recall the sheer bliss and excitement
on the faces of those arriving to the strip (NOT as is
the "strip" club, rather, the "strip" of the boulevard)
in Las Vegas from the darkness of the desert for the
first time by car, or a child's face lighting up in the
stroller when being wheeled into Disneyland for the
first time, or a devout elderly Catholic woman landing
in Jerusalem realizing her lifelong pilgrimage to trace
Jesus' footsteps in the Via de la Rosa. You get the
point…?

Just as Buddhism teaches us, respect any and all living
things- You never know if you'll come back as a toad
in your next incarnation; and we don't know if that
can actually happen of course, but it's better to be
safe than sorry and cover all bases… JK ("Just
Kidding").

Being respectful of living things should be natural, not take any special effort, but it is also worth noting that all living organisms are interconnected in the food chain somehow (*"six degrees of separation"* within the food cycle and that of life itself).

To illustrate that interconnectivity and reliance, recall the bee colony collapse epidemic...? Well, a combination of factors; several harsh winters when the epidemic was first noticed just over a decade ago (it first made mainstream headlines in 2006), increased attacks by bee parasites, exposure to some modified and far stronger agricultural pesticides perhaps and, believe it or not, bees worrying themselves to death by some, led to the devastating decline in bee populations. Conspiracies aside, according to Global Research, since 2006, the bee population has declined by up to 70% in some places, such as Iowa and other high-yielding honey states- The Dakotas, Montana, Minnesota; essentially, the Northern Plains and Midwestern states, while in warmer locales, such as Florida and California, the decline (of which figures vary, but all point to 40-50%) is also very significant, though not as steep. And of course there's a cool acronym for this phenomenon- CCD, or the honeybee "Colony Collapse Disorder" (NO SHIT!).

This sharp decline in honeybees has been linked with a change in the foraging behavior in which queen bees and their colonies respond to by sending out their young, largely inexperienced, bee workers to forage for food, hence magnifying an already bad situation and making it exponentially worse for the future bee population prospects simply because the novice bees clearly cannot successfully match their more adept and skillful counterparts in bringing back the appropriate amount of food needed even for just the sustenance of today's colonies, let alone their growth...

Confusing...? Never mind. All you need to know is that bees are essential for our survival (illustrating our cross-species interdependency, or the "*six degrees of separation*" in the food cycle I mentioned). They pollinate an estimate $40 billion worth of our agricultural produce each year according to Newsweek and, as reminded by USDA Agriculture Secretary Tom Vilsack, more than 130 types of fruits and vegetables that make up a nutritious diet are cross pollinated by honeybees.

In all, "commercial bees" (these are the "professionals" or "moneymakers", insofar as bee life goes, of course...) along with their counterparts comprising the wild bee population (that would be the freeloaders of the bee population profile, it's dependents) are responsible for the pollination of an estimated 80% of all food crops in the United States. That being the case, you should be nice to them; that's all I'm saying...

Also related to our relationship with the animal kingdom is pet ownership, or, more importantly, companionship. So many positive effects have been attributed to pets in our midst, I won't even be able to cite them all. From comforting children with Down syndrome, to providing companionship for the elderly and so much more. In a more fundamental and intrinsic sense, the simple truth that pets just make you happy. The manner in which humans interact with animals (don't get any ideas…), brings forth solace, peace, calm and happiness.

These interactions also result in smiling, among other physical reactions, all of which culminate in the same thing- The release of endorphins, our body's natural opiates, as well as other "feel good" chemicals in the brain including dopamine, oxytocin, prolactin and norepinephrine. All of these are a part of our primal defensive mechanism to combat stress, relieve pain and promote overall, good health which, in turn, leads to a longer life, lived better.

By the way, in case you're wondering, other activities which release similar endorphins are intense exercise (one of the many benefits, of course), eating hot peppers (yup, that's why Mexicans are always happy!), laughing (that's why comedians live long) and eating dark chocolate (that's why my mom is, well, never mind…).

Side note: Just to get this straight- If hot peppers release endorphins (they do) and nutmeg can cause hallucinations (it can), what do we need synthetic drugs for...? Either way, do humanity a favor and stay away from the bath salts.

When embracing or cradling a child, the same happens. In some religions, it is believed that a child has a pure white aura above them (just as the most pious and righteous people do) and that this aura contains good energy which permeates to the person holding the child, thus making him/ her feel better- The result of the same reasons noted above; the release of endorphins. That said, we do all have electro-magnetic fields which emit energy and aura photography does point to that chaste, pure, clean aura surrounding babies.

Unfortunately for the rest of us, it's all downhill from birth so, to put it mildly, your own aura (and mine as well, don't worry... in this world, unless living in a bubble, that aura starts getting blemished at a very young age unfortunately...) is not only tainted, but most likely tarnished beyond repair. Whatever the cause, whatever the reason; the effects of pets AND babies are similar and extremely positive for a myriad reasons so that's that...

As long as we're in a quasi-theological discussion, let's address rituals or religious rituals or age-old cultural practices. I have always held the belief that, if such doctrines or tenets related to how humans conduct themselves (how to prepare and eat food, what they, how they purify themselves among countless other rituals), withstand the test of time, there is in fact a logical and rational explanation for them.

Side note: As long as we're on religious grounds, I have always found it interesting that, in so many completely unrelated religions, the practice of purifying one's soul; NOT the habitual ritual of cleaning oneself (which almost universally uses water as the cleansing medium) rather the more "robust" purification needed when one reaches adulthood, gets married or is facing a grave ailment or some demons lurking within, the use of hallucinogens is both common and prevalent. Almost every older culture at least one form of hallucinogen to be used for the above listed occasions; usually in administered in a very ceremonial and traditional manner. .

Just as whether the "aura" discussed above is a sign of chastity and divine purity, or just an a representation electromagnetic field, these ceremonies involving hallucinogens can also be regarded and revered as the work of God, delivered to us mortals by Dervishes, Shamans, Monks, Rabbis, Chiefs, priests and other messengers. Or simply a way for us to enter an altered state, lose our grip on reality, sense of balance; both physical and emotional, or any other sensory deprivation brought on by fasting, deliberate exhaustion, physical pain, vertigo or any combination of these and other symptoms.

Almost all religions use fasting as a way to seek redemption and to repent for our sins. The Catholics have lent to teach the same doctrine and so forth. Many use physical punishment- In some cases, such as Sharia Law, the penance is administered by enforcers; in others, such as Opus Dei, a secretive devout Catholic sect founded about a century ago in Spain, it is self-inflicted.

Other religions, mostly the more introspective Eastern ones, like the Buddhists, Hindus and Taoists, as do I, prefer meditation, repetitive chanting or simple silence to get into "the zone" by. Jews practice an endless array of rituals- They engage in repetitive practices that become second nature, they learn and pray until virtual collapse, they fast, they jump in freezing waters at dawn, some even stop their cars and get out in the middle of the street as if they just started rolling at a rave (almost anyone in Manhattan or Los Angeles can attest to that phenomenon...). For the record, while I am in fact an "MOT" ("Member of Tribe"), a stupid term denoting Jewish affiliation conceived by American Jews, I don't practice any of this... Bad Jew!

In other ancient civilizations, indigenous cultures and traditional religions, other "instruments" are employed to cause a loss of balance, a blurring of reality or other form of sensory deprivation- The Shamans of Amazonia deep in the Peruvian jungle prepare tea with Ayuhuasca, The Yemenites chew Ga'at for endless sessions, the Indians make a "tent sauna" and smoke Peyote and the "Twirling Dervishes" of the Zoroastrians do just that, twirl... All resulting in the same imbalance of the body and mind.

Back to those traditions and rituals that withstood the test of time. Chinese women eat pig's knuckles during pregnancy; they've done so for a millennia. Potassium is a mineral that plays a significant role in maintaining the balance of fluids and electrolytes in our cells. It is also important for sending nerve impulses and helping your muscles contract. Vomiting and nausea, both common during pregnancy, contribute to the depletion of potassium. Also, during pregnancy, your blood volume expands by about 50%, so in order to keep the right chemical balance, more potassium is needed. Guess what...Pigs knuckles are extremely rich in potassium. Simple.

Jewish dietary laws are among the most complicated on our planet... That said, most make sense, especially given the time frame of when they were scribed. Jews are not allowed to eat milk and meat together because "...you should not cook a calf in its mother's milk". That's a nice theological explanation, but the truth is that milk and meat are the two toughest and longest foods to digest, if both are eaten in significant amounts.

So, while a cheeseburger might not be a good example, just recall the last time you had a burger complemented by a milkshake, then the gastric mayhem that ensued shortly thereafter. Another example is even simpler- Jews don't eat pork because they're filthy animals that eat all the crap on the ground (although swine, in certain forms tastes damn good, I must admit...).

Similarly, Jews don't eat crustaceans (shrimp, lobster, crab, scallops, squid and lobster, etc.). The reason is simple, they only eat the filth and refuse off the ocean's floor. So, all that's true, on top of which back in the day there was no way to refrigerate or keep these ocean critters fresh and you how they smell and what havoc they wreak on your stomach just a few hours after being harvested from the seas and not kept chilled...

Lastly on this matter, remember the bovine spongiform encephalopathy outbreak? Of course you don't! Actually, you do, but under it's more common name, Mad Cow disease. Anyhoo, BSE is caused by a misfolded protein called a prion. A British and Irish inquiry into the disease concluded it was caused by cattle, which are of course herbivores, being fed the remains of other cattle. BSE-infected animals were introduced to our food chain before controls on high-risk offal (also known as "variety meats", "pluck", or "organ meats" are the internal organs and entrails of a butchered animal) were enacted in 1989. In all, 180,000 cows in England and 300,000 cows in France were identified with the disease and 4.4 million were slaughtered during the disease eradication program. Guess what…? Kosher cows were not affected at all because of the dietary restrictions.

Unrelated to Mad Cow, or BSE, the manner in which animals are slaughtered is also an interesting point to ponder. Regular slaughterhouses have a narrow labyrinth the cattle are prodded through on their way to being electrocuted. Today, we all know that the cows in line seeing their brethren electrified to death become tense, fearful and release the three Major Stress Hormones associated with *"fight or flight"* scenarios; adrenaline, cortisol and norepinephrine, into the bloodstream. Under kashrut (kosher) laws, the "shochet" (or, "slaughterer") slices the cow's main artery and it bleeds to death quickly and alone. As such, there are none of the "anticipatory poisons" released under conventional slaughtering circumstances and, quite frankly, beef without these poisons injected into the bloodstream is far safer, better and healthier for us.

In short, kosher laws, just like the Muslim halal laws and the Chinese example provided above all make perfect sense and there is good reasoning behind each such mandate; whether it be a cultural ritual or a religious edict.

As long as we're on religion, let's stay in the neighborhood. Always seek solace, peace and serenity. This means a ton of things- Don't look for fights and don't relish on confrontation (or, as often refried to today, "drama"). Rather, try to resolve misunderstandings and disagreements by seeking mature dialogue and other peaceful resolutions whenever and as much as possible.

In a physical and biorhythm sense, find your own balance as well. Find out when are your peak performance hours are, in what attire you are most comfortable, down to the lighting, temperature, background music and seat you recline on. Comfort of body is essential to achieve peace of mind. Just as pain stings us, curbs our movements and inhibits our quality of life; conversely, physical discomfort enables us to perform at our peak, have a clear mind, to be uninterrupted, even make us feel so free, as if we can fly.

So, whatever it takes and how much you have to sacrifice to make it happen, it is imperative you do this; to improve yourself and to be better for those who depend on you.

Practice patience- It truly is a virtue; especially in the immediacy of today. My son ordered a motorcycle and I cannot tell you how disappointed he was when we "checked out" and he learned it'll take a whole three days to get delivered. I remember when ordering a couch used to take 4-6 months to get by ship from Italy and this little shit is whining about three days... This instant gratification is devoid of the build-up, the expectation and the anticipation of the big arrival of whatever it is you're buying or receiving. As with many things these days, these feelings no longer exist.

This expectation of immediacy and "instant everything" manifests itself elsewhere in today's life, just recall the last time you couldn't pick up your ten year-old girl's phone call...? I do. She gives the word "stalker" a new meaning, time and time again; with a few seconds in between. And when we do finally talk, her questioning put even the C.I.A.'s interrogation tactics to shame. It's not her fault- Like Pavlov's dogs, that's how she, and everyone else these days, were (and continue to be) conditioned. That said, it does lead to unreasonable expectations, at times even a sense of entitlement that you must curb. These presumptions & assumptions must be sensibly managed, not nourish or enabled in any way, shape or form.

This phenomenon of "immediacy" is of course not just relegated to our children- Try not responding to a call or text someone deems important; whether it's your mate/lover, boss, family member, friend or anyone else that is relatively close to you. And it matters little if you're driving, in the toilet, having sex or in court- You are expected to be reachable 24/7 and as responsive at midnight as you are expected to be at noon. It's a travesty and a true shame to our collective wellbeing.

The notion of good things come to those who wait is trivial in our world, but always remember that there is a natural order to anything and everything in life and all that we do. Just as juggling the grocery bags, while trying to close the trunk and fidgeting with the keys to lock the car or open the house, things always need to get done in a certain order. When that order isn't followed, in many cases, Murphy's Law ensues and everything seems to go wrong or fall apart. Sometimes the consequences are diminutive; sometimes they are dreadful. Whatever the case at hand is, try to accomplish what you need in the order needed.

Meditate to open your mind, release your body and free your soul, steam to detoxify yourself and dip into a sauna to cleanse your flesh. Whenever I am lucky enough to be at a nice resort or spa, I indulge myself with these pleasures of the flesh. They truly do a remarkable job in both purifying and rejuvenating our bodies.

Then, walk. Just walk. With no purpose in mind at first, just for the sport of it. Shake your hands as you walk. Release your limbs, regenerate your lungs & stretch your muscles. Walk around the block, walk the dog, walk during your lunchtime, take the stairs instead of the elevator or escalator, perhaps even enjoy some nature and get some sun by hiking. The sun, by the way, has both negative and positive effects on our health. Remember "Forest Gump"…?

A little sun exposure is good for our "Third Eye" (that's why believers open their mouths pointed upwards every morning for a few minutes; to let the sun awaken that Third Eye). Beyond the realm of the paranormal, the sun is also a principal source of vitamin D3 and mutagen. One thing that is imperative to remember is to stretch- Stretching is extremely important to do before all forms of physical activity as our elasticity starts to degenerate almost instantaneously, stretching warms up the muscles and helps prevent injury.

As long as we're outdoors, don't forget to work the land from time to time. Aaron David Gordon who founded Ha'poel Ha'tzair, a movement influenced by Leo Tolstoy which exalted the benefits of laboring the land, so much so he in effect made a religion of labor. No need to take it to that degree of course, but trimming the hedges, mowing the lawn and especially planting (much more so with your kids, provided you have any. If you don't, borrow someone's kid/s for a day; it's a great experience they should not miss).

And yet even more on the outdoors, take the family to the beach. Sometimes, go by yourself for a short escape, to re-charge and refill those batteries. Take a stroll on the beach, kick the sand, rush into the waves, collect seashells, build sandcastles, breath in the air, taste the salt or just watch the sunset. The ocean; and the forest, and the mountain, and the hill, and the valley, and the cliff, and the gorge, and the desert, and the and the river, stream and lake and all that is in between that is the grace of nature and the majesty of its beauty. An extension of this is camping- An amazing, but unfortunately almost extinct tradition that bonds friends and family like little else in life.

Road trips fall into the same bucket and even feature family sing-alongs and games on the way (ok, some discourse every now and then, but the family that fights together, stays together). Just watch the films "Grand Canyon", "The Bucket List" or "The Fundamentals of Caring" and you'll get the point; hell, even "Driving Miss Daisy" and "Thelma & Louis" illustrate the camaraderie and bonding that only a road trip can foster; whether by one long trip or a lifetime of short drives.

A few years back, I took my two kids, a boy of 8 and a girl of 6 at the time, along with my stepson and we embarked on a road trip just short of two weeks. Starting from L.A., we traversed seven states, almost a dozen national parks (as well as countless state and local ones), endless driving and an unforgettable trip. We laughed, we cried, we sang, we talked, we fought and, yes, we farted- It was priceless and the memory of a lifetime; except for those pieces of driftwood I picked up at Jackson Lake just south of Yellowstone we transported in the back seat of my car which my son rammed his face into. Only once, but he'll never let me forget it. In all fairness, when that unfortunate incident transpired, I inquired about the condition of the wooden slab prior to my son's wellbeing, so I reckon I deserve it. You see, the world has a funny way to keep things in balance and our life has a funny way of keeping us in check; Karma at it's very best.

Always keep in mind, the journey is no less as important as the destination; and not just when you're headed to a rave in the forest, desert, or, if in Thailand or India or Brazil or Uruguay or Greece or Croatia or Estonia or Israel; the beach. Yes, I said it, Ibiza and Miami are old news.

Traveling abroad is quintessential for intellectual growth, to foster understanding and the acceptance of other cultures and peoples. If we are to live in harmony on this planet, it is a must. So whether by Birthright, the military, as a diplomat, volunteer or missionary work, the Peace Corps, Merchant Marines, Civilian Conservation Corps or just a good ol' family vacation, try to expose you and yours to as much as you can as often as possible.

Given the availability of time and funds, you should try & plan these excursions and expeditions to the far reaches of mother earth. If the wallet ain't fat, keep it closer to home, but if you can, travel to the ends of the earth. It's sad to know how little Americans travel, compared to the rest of the world. I'm not comparing low income families here to the upper socioeconomic echelon of Europe or Asia; I am comparing citizens of the Western industrialized world of similar income prorated in terms of travel.

Maybe it's because we don't get as much vacation time as our European counterparts. Maybe it's because the United States is so big and offers such a variety of different cultures and landscapes, we don't feel the necessity or urge to travel abroad. Maybe it is because we are so damn far away from everyone else; with the possible exception of Australia, New Zealand and South Africa, in terms of countries of the same ilk. Whatever the reason, or combination thereof, we Americans just don't get out there that often.

To illustrate how little we travel, on our best year, just under 30 million overseas trips were taken by 14.6 million Americans. If we omit business travel, overseas study programs, that number drops to just 11.6 million people, or about 3.5% of the population. If you exclude our neighbors to the north and south;

Canada and Mexico, the picture is far worse. And if you deduct the very significant amount of expats from large communities going back to the motherland for a home/ family visit, such as Britain, Ireland, Poland, Russia, Ukraine, Israel, Armenia, China, The Philippines, South Korea, Thailand most of Central America, on top of the aforementioned two nations, the numbers are minuscule compared to the foreign travel rate from populations in other developed countries.

The notion sometimes is that they all come here, so we can "experience" these cultures in our domestic Chinatowns, Thaitowns, Koreatowns (or "K-Towns"), or the "Little Tokyo/ Saigon/Italy/Greece/Armenia/Ethiopia/ you fill in the blank neighborhoods or concentrations of said nationalities, but it is dead wrong.

Just as much as you cannot experience Paris (the real one, not the one in Texas- Why do we have towns named after major cities is truly beyond me) by going to the eponymous hotel in Las Vegas, nor experience England by visiting the London Bridge in Havasu, Arizona, or Denmark by way of Solvang, California, you cannot experience those same places by driving to a nearby expat community strip of restaurants and shops.

Side note: The Chinese, as the Chinese do, actually took the Vegas model of replicating cities and

international landmarks and, as the Chinese do,
boosted, upgraded and refined this replication (to an
art form of course) in building no less than ELEVEN
cities literally "copied" from the rest of the world. Ha!
And you thought designer bags were an issue; they're
knocking off entire cities now!!! What's next, a replica
of every human too, so we all have a Chinese identical
twin (just in case we break...?). Between the rapid
progress of AI, us becoming Robot-bitches and this
shit, God knows what's worse and where we'll wind
up.

But we digress... The Business Insider actually did a
spread on these Chinese replicas ("same, same, but
different"), which include the historic Austrian Alpine
village, Hallstatt, is copied in its entirety just outside
Guangdong. There is also the "Florentia Village"
(why couldn't they just call it, "Florentine", I haven't a
clue...) in, where else, but near the port city of
Tianjin (perhaps an ode to Marco Polo), replete with
canals, fountains and mosaics as well as "local" shops
like Gucci and Prada. A few hours outside of
Shanghai, you'll find the town of Tianducheng, which
is, what else...? A copycat of Paris, including a 354ft
(108m) Eiffel Tower. Across the river from Hong
Kong is the "Overseas Chinese Town East (OCT)",
an ecosystem theme park with a man-made lake and
an entire district modeled after Interlaken,
Switzerland. There's more, but you get the point...

Back to true travel- A good place to start are the Seven Wonders of the World. Of course there has to be discourse about which World Heritage Sites comprise this list, so we have two lists- The traditional and the "new" wonders; and of course both have modifications so they're more apropos for today's PC climate... Combining the lists, they include; The Great Pyramid of Giza in Egypt, the only remaining site from the OG (or "ancient") list of wonders, The Coliseum in Rome, Italy, The Great Wall of China, Hagia Sofia- at first a Greek Orthodox patriarchal basilica, then an imperial mosque and now a museum in Istanbul, Turkey, Stonehenge in England, Machu Picchu in the Andes of Peru, the Taj Mahal palace and mausoleum in Agra, India, the Empire State Building in New York the Golden Gate Bridge in San Francisco, the moai statues (900 no less) in Rapa Nui aka Easter Island, the Terra Cotta soldiers of Xi'an, China, the ancient Khmer capital of Angkor Wat in Krong Siem Reap, Cambodia, Victoria Falls between Zambia and Zimbabwe, the Great Barrier Reef in Australia, the Grand Canyon in Arizona, the Sydney Opera House, the Mayan pyramid, Chichen Itza in the eastern Yucatán, the Old City of Jerusalem in Israel, Iguacu Falls adjoining Brazil and Argentina, Christ the Redeemer Statue overlooking Rio de Janeiro and the Aurora Borealis (or "Northern Lights") occurring in a belt centered 1,550mi (2,500km) away from the magnetic north pole, called the "auroral zone", which extends across northern Scandinavia, Iceland, Greenland, Canada, Alaska and Siberia.

The United Nations' UNESCO "World Heritage
Site" list includes 1073 sites; of which 832 are labeled
as "Cultural", 206 as "Natural" and 35 labeled as
"Mixed" in 167 countries, so feel free to go ape shit;
traveling is one expense you will never regret (unlike
those ridiculous shoes, purses or that bottle service
table you got for New Year's at a nightclub).

Whatever you do and wherever you go, do NOT let
the millennials just "document" the trip, as they often
do with their Snapchat, Instagram, Twitter, Facebook
(only if you're REALLY OLD) or whatever the flavor
of the day is and make sure these critters actually
"experience" these glorious marvels of nature and
magnificent manmade wonders you have worked so
hard to get them to visit. Let them take their two
hundred selfies, but make sure they also go on a hike.

Choose an activity from the vast (and timeless) menu
of the global physical arts disciplines; Aikido, Qi
Gong, Wing Chun, Wushu, tai chi, Kempo, Kyūdō,
Kendo, Muay Thai, capoeira, judo, karate, grappling,
Sambo, Tae Kwon Do, Krav Maga, kung fu or any
number of other alternatives. Note: NOT boxing or
kickboxing, unless you're a professional; it's just too
dangerous.

Any of these fighting arts (what an oxymoron...) will
help that heart of yours, your stamina, invigorate you,
relieve some of that stress, anxiety & pressure boiling

inside of you (sometimes…), make you feel & look better and assist your mental and emotional wellbeing in countless other ways. Besides, any of these will introduce you to a new batch of people & help your social life. It will also instill some discipline, help you focus (not to mention, fight) better.

If you're a lover, not a fighter, then pick a sport- Golf, tennis (yes, I'm white; well, sort of…), soccer (only outdoor- the only soccer there is), baseball, softball, volleyball (beach or court), basketball (or even just practice drills for any of the aforementioned) scuba diving, parachuting, paragliding, heli-skiing, skiing, snowboarding, sailing, kayaking, surfing, windsurfing, rowing, water-skiing, wake-boarding, Moto X, quads, cycling (mountain, BMX, 10-speed, 12-speed, even a 50's Schwinn or Raleigh Chopper; whatever gets your rocks off).

Speaking of lovers, the groundbreaking and pioneering research of William H. Masters & Virginia E. Johnson did a remarkable job, under tremendous duress (or many shades…) mind you, into the nature of human sexual response (as well as the diagnosis and treatment of sexual disorders and dysfunctions, but that's not the focus here), spanning no less than five decades (I'm they could have done it in half the time, but why…). This lifelong commitment (NOT the Sexual Revolution, not feminism, nor most definitely porn or internet dating) is the single most important and seminal event affecting how we view, and enjoy, sex; especially given our nation's

Puritanical roots. Masters and Johnson's trials and tribulations have been depicted in the four-season television series "Masters of Sex" which aired on Showtime (what the fuck happened to Netflix???).

I am no advocate of "whoredome" or promiscuity but I do believe people need to let go of taboos and learn to enjoy their (and other's, as the case may be) bodies. If it is between consenting adults (notice I didn't write "two"), it's fair game and normal (and if someone is an idiot, we get to see them on Discovery's reality series "Untold stories of the E.R." and learn why we shouldn't stick a light bulb in that particular orifice and just use a flashlight…).

Many people have told me this and I myself believe it ardently- "*Be a lady or gentleman in public, but be a whore (woman or man(whore) in bed*".

To illustrate just how little we knew about our own bodies, while I won't start listing the low percentage and sad state of female orgasms until just a few decades ago, nor the ridiculous and infantile questions some high school students ask about sex simply because their schools and parents opted NOT to talk about it, electing to avoid the subject altogether (because it doesn't exist if we don't talk about it, right???), I will tell you one tidbit of history related to the subject; and I shit you not, it is true.

During the 19th century, just over one hundred years and some decades ago, "female hysteria" was an actual, and very common, medical diagnosis, especially afflicting women. These women exhibited an array of symptoms, including faintness, insomnia, shortness of breath, a bloated abdomen, irritability and an overall "tendency to cause trouble" (yes, described in those precise words).

Using a variety of treatments including hypnosis, sometimes even a forced hysterectomy and, in severe cases, a life relegated to an insane asylum, the brilliant medical minds of the day found a new, fairly simple treatment of this troubling ailment. Their doctors simply manually stimulated (or, master bated…) the women to climax- Now, THAT'S what I call "Obama Care"! In fact, the doctors' hands got so fatigued after so many daily sessions that, eventually and in many different early manifestations, they ultimately invented the vibrator (yes- just to give their hands a rest…).

Lastly on the subject and despite popular belief (it ain't THAT popular because nobody knows my ass), while I am NOT a sexist by any measure, I have to share one of my all-time favorite one-liners with you (but DON'T judge me, please…):

Question: Why do women fake orgasms…?

Answer: Because they think we care.

Start a workout out regimen- With weights, with friends, Stair Master, jogging, running (flat and/or steps), take an aerobic or step class, shit, even Zumba; just move. And remember to partake in both aerobic, or cardiovascular, exercises (those sustained exercises that stimulate and strengthen the heart and lungs, thereby improving the body's use of oxygen and, in turn, your metabolism) as well as anaerobic work outs (weight lifting and so forth; exercises that are intense enough to cause lactate to form, thus promoting strength, speed and power by increasing muscle mass). Note: NEVER football or rugby as a hobby; that's just stupid, especially at our age... All the same benefits from just above apply here too. Just remember to stretch and always warm up.

Maybe take a dance class- Ballroom, swing, salsa, merengue, samba, cha cha, paso doble, electronic music even breakdancing if you can; whatever your style, just move a little. You got it... The same benefits.

For related reasons- A sense of fulfillment, achievement, purpose, even to build a future nest egg (for either a rainy day or for retirement), start a collection hobby. These are virtually endless- Stamps, coins, Chinaware, match boxes, watches, gems, ties, purses, couture, wines, sports cards, beer mugs, shot glasses, teaspoons, snuff bottles, ceramics, pots frames, old typewriters, goggles, eye glasses, jeans, hats, masks, t-shirts, key chains, postcards, stickers, refrigerator magnets, figurines, mugs, plates, license plates (miniature or real), bones, taxidermy, it's fucking endless, indeed…

Indulge yourself and be social by attending some rock, hip hop, pop or classical philharmonic concerts, the opera, theatre plays and musicals, go to a stand-up comedy club, a ballgame or watch some movies (in the cinema, like they were meant to be watched- I just discovered a still (very) active drive-in theatre, just like back in the 50's; fucking genius!. Insofar as silent movie theaters go, you won't be as lucky as they aren't that abundant these days. Actually, there's only one left in the world; right here in Los Angeles, but it only plays silent movies once a week so plan ahead; whatever you wanted, but never gave yourself the pleasure of actually doing. Just remember, ALWAYS within reason and within budget.

Have a social game night every now and then; with family or friends, on a regular basis or whenever the circumstances permit. Board games- Go (yes, the same Go from many pages ago…), Rummikub, chess, backgammon, checkers, bingo night (if you're that desperate) card games- Baccarat, Pai Gow, Rummy (both Gin Rummy and Oklahoma Gin), poker, bridge, blackjack, just don't be a fool…

Join an association or a club or fraternity, of any age. Whether a church choir, religious study group, band, hiking or ballroom dancing club, the Boy Scouts, Girl Scouts, Harvard Club, a think tank, Toast Masters, Neighborhood Watch, The Harvard Club, Algonquin, whatever... We all have an innate need for a sense of belonging and these will replenish some of that lost socialization of our time.

I'm sorry, but I for one never got the racing thing; cars, monster trucks, figure eight, mud bog, NASCAR, Formula I & III, speedboats, catamaran, Hobby Cat, jet skis, sailing, ice racing, snowmobiling, Motocross, Supercross, Motorcycle GP (500cc or 750cc), Superbike, horses, greyhounds, chickens, crickets... but if any of these work for you; whether as a participant or for gambling purposes, go for it, but remember what's at stake; again, regardless if you're a participant or waging a bet.

Paint, draw, illustrate, sculpt, mold, make clay pottery, masks, jewelry, photograph nature, nudes, still life; in color or black and white; posterized, sepia-toned, highlighted, framed or manipulated in a myriad other ways, assemble a mosaic, a collage, or create your own visual palate with a multimedia work of art. Whatever your preferred style is- Classical, figurative, impressionist, abstract, cubist, art nouveau, beaux arts, art deco, or modernist, art brings solace, peace and balance to every facet of the soul and mind; that much, I can personally attest to. So go ahead and explore colors, textures and shapes. Experiment with different types of paints and raw materials. Investigate different techniques, applications, genres and subject matters.

Listen to the music you love sometimes, not just what your kids, mate or parents prefer, in most cases, dictate. Hell, make a "mix tape" for different moods and different purposes (yup, just like the 80's, only now it's a digital playlist- It seems nothing is tangible anymore; everything is digital, augmented, virtual... Isn't anything sacred people???).

Sing- As loud and as often (and as bad, if that's the case) as you can. Not just in the shower or in the car- Go to a karaoke club once in a blue moon with friends, family or work colleagues and embarrass yourself publicly; it'll only do you good.

Expand your horizons. Whether it's by traveling, food, music, film, sex, sports, a hobby, an interest; anything that will give you a sense of purpose, that which motivates and fulfills you and gives you satisfaction and a sense of achievement. Lastly on the subject, while we exalted the benefits of planning, it is sometimes good to just let go, be spontaneous and impulsive and spice up life a bit.

Similarly- Talk less, listen more. You learn by listening; talking only feeds your ego. Succinctly expressed by Benjamin Franklin when he said: *"Great talkers, little doers"*.

And when you do absolutely have to talk, don't lie- *"If you don't lie, you have nothing to remember"*. You have a clear conscious and mind; to do far more important things and pursue more worthwhile endeavors.

On a related note, *"Don't bite more than you can chew"*, or *"Don't write a check you cannot cover…"*. Speaking of biting and chewing, remember- *"In life, sometimes you're the dog and sometimes you're the fire hydrant"*. Know which it is at any given time, adjust and adapt to it to the best of your ability and execute what is needed to attain your desired goal, as always should be the priority to do…

When you fuck up, be a mensch and apologize. Simple. There is no shame in modesty, however, there is much vice in arrogance, pretentiousness and entitlement. Originating from a prayer of confession and now often used in legal jargon, the Latin phrase *"Mea Culpa"* (*"through my fault"*) perfectly embodies the concepts of both admittance of guilt and that of seeking redemption, both of which display humility and bring solace.

Likewise, always acknowledge and express genuine appreciation and gratitude. Reciprocate in kind. Try to minimize your expectations to avoid your own disappointment and others' feelings of guilt. Remember, *"When nothing goes right, go left..."* (LOL/JK).

Related to both of the above, take a day of quiet reflection to review your life- Where you and where you want to be. If it is elsewhere, which measures or what path can you embark on to bring you closer to that goal. Evaluate your children's lives and do the same.

Remember, very few people have the intellectual capacity, physical stamina, mental tenacity and emotional stability to become a brain surgeon or astronaut, but everyone has at least one thing they're damn good at; or, at the very least, better than most.

Then review your relationships, only the one which are important to you. Decide if those are where they should be and what can be done to remedy those that are not in balance or your desired "condition". Whether a rift resulted from sibling rivalry, a sandwich child syndrome, being the youngest or being born to an elderly parent incapable of many of the physical activities one would expect said parent to engage in together, a new spouse (the kid/s or the parent/s...) that tore the family apart or those relationships distanced by misplaced anger, unnecessary envy, a feeling of abandonment, lack of attention, care or love, even violence; to an extent, try to do your part in rectifying whatever you can to the degree a particular relationship can be restored. Remember, once someone is gone, they are gone forever. That said, do whatever you can WITHOUT humiliating yourself, insulting the other/s or not addressing that which requires resolution and closure. Otherwise, it's not healthy and absolutely no good; for anyone.

Be kind and benevolent to all living things, much more so to those who are in distress, your dependents and those who look up to you.

Treat everyone as equal; prejudices and bigotry originate from ignorance or arrogance. Either "I don't know you, so I fear you", or "I don't know you, but I'm better than you". Treat others exactly as you wish others to treat you.

Be a fair, respectful, humble and responsible member of your community. Say "Hello", "Please" and "Thank you". Insofar as civic duties go, become engaged and an actively contributing member of your community.

Join (or form) the Neighborhood Watch group. Maybe plan a BBQ, baseball game or movie night and invite your neighbors to a meal once in a while or party you're throwing. Try to turn your neighborhood of strangers to a community of friends. Home and its vicinity will be more welcoming, the kids will be safer; besides, you never know when you'll run out of coffee, milk or sugar and, as noted long ago; "*It takes a village…*", so build one…

Volunteer, donate and do some charitable work. Get your hands dirty once in a while- You'll meet new people, help out folks in need and you will be reminded and appreciate just how lucky you are REAL quick. THE most fulfilled AND revered people I have ever had the pleasure of befriending or just meeting, were these.

A distant relative of mine was such a mensch of a man. Itzik (or "Isaac") was his name. He was a psychologist and his entire life was devoted to helping others- From healing the wounds and teaching coping strategies to soldiers with PTSD ("Post Traumatic Stress Disorder") in different countries, different armies and different wars; to mentoring the most menacing felons incarcerated in maximum security prisons across California in facing their demons, comprehending the gravity and damage of their crimes and expressing genuine repentance for the evil they have inflicted and the pain they have spread.

These are the greatest contributors to the human race: The first responders- Firefighters, COPS, EMT's, nurses and doctors; those enlisted in the National Guard and the soldiers serving in our military. Those who abandon all wanton in lieu of helping their fellow man. They readily offer their time, talent and knowledge, often at great sacrifice, to improve, rehabilitate and revive the wellbeing and the lives of others at times of suffering; irrespective if these are the result of the damage caused by nature's fury or a the atrocities of man. A true utilitarian approach to humanity. They embody the difference between being successful and being significant.

Those who seek justice and fight the darkest evils of mankind- Ruthless totalitarian despots who intentionally inflict famine, deny their populace the very basic of human rights, even murder their own countrymen in savage and brutal ways that inflict irreparable damage for generations to come. Those who engage in human trafficking, child pornography, forced child labor or the coerced militia enlistment of juveniles.

Those who manipulate others, even send them to their death, just to serve their own sinister agendas. The poachers, the pillagers, the slave traders, the rapists and the abusers; in their endless shades. Those who imprison others to placate their demented fetishes, abduct the innocent to appease their deranged perversions and kidnap, hold hostage or assault the helpless for financial gain. Those who sabotage liberty, hold captive and bound their fellow man to quell their own evil obsessions and inflict their vicious tyranny.

The deranged minds, distorted reality, nefarious scheming, twisted logic, vile intentions and the necessary annihilation of one's moral compass needed to commit such heinous atrocities, dispense such pain and leave nothing but carnage in their path are the absolute perversion of humanity. And they must be stopped and defeated. Those who aid in battling these ferocious, enduring and suffocating wars are the saints of our race and embody the pinnacle of humanity.

A sentiment first conceived in ancient times by Agricola Tacitus and later popularized by John F Kennedy during the Bay of Pigs invasion 1962 says it all… "*Victory has a hundred fathers and defeat is an orphan*".

"*Evil triumphs when good men do nothing*"- The words of Elie Wiesel, a Romanian-born American Jewish writer (of 57 books nonetheless, most notable of which is "Night", recounting his captivity at the Auschwitz and Buchenwald concentration camps), professor, political activist, Nobel Laureate and Holocaust survivor. These very few and very simple, yet equally powerful words that resonate with every atrocity that is committed and each victim it afflicts. In short, "… *if we lose our principles, we invite chaos*".

As the aforementioned Dennis Prager insightfully points out, "… *Courage is the rarest of human qualities*". Truer words were seldom spoken.

If you witness an injustice or crime being committed, strive to remedy, rectify and help however you can. Don't just be a bystander- Get involved and pursue justice. Whether it's bullying or embezzlement you are privy to, find your inner Atticus Finch and contribute to tip the scales of justice in the right direction.

Side note: Atticus Finch is the protagonist in Harper Lee's 1960 Pulitzer Prize-Winning novel, "To Kill a Mockingbird" and the perfect embodiment of this type of man. A big screen adaptation of the book was released two years later showcasing a brilliant Academy Award-winning performance by Gregory Peck in the lead role. The Atticus Finch character has been voted "The greatest hero of all American cinema" by the American Film Institute.

In the movie, Atticus Finch famously said "*The one thing that doesn't abide by majority rule is a person's courage*".

Disclaimer: When you do act to seek justice or engage in the pursuit of the truth, it is imperative to be rational and employ both caution and logic; e.g. my

70-something year-old mommy should NOT give chase to an armed robber and I should steer clear of even thinking about trying to stop a suspect being pursued by the police in a high-speed chase when I'm in the car with a bunch of kids coming back from my son's baseball game.

Show empathy to your fellow man in distress. Whether the suffering is physical or emotional; and regardless if they're close to you or not. My father took in a teenager who was living on his own at 16, two thousand miles from home; with no family, nor any money. He worked tirelessly and was dedicated beyond reproach. Then we found out he was an addict. My dad sent him to rehab. A few months following his return, he was invited for an interview at a major record label. With my dad's help and backing (and fibbing…), he secured the job.

Within three years, he was head of marketing and promotion at one of the world's largest entertainment conglomerates. Today, he is happily married, has two kids and is at the summit of the film industry. A beautiful story which would not have been possible had someone not cared enough to step up and give the kid a home and a chance.

While nothing compared to the contribution of Dr. Charles Mutua Mully through his charitable organization, "Mully Children's Family", as documented in the film "Mully" which is certainly worthy of a watch, it is a small step towards a better planet. As taught in The Talmud, the body of Jewish law, "… *whoever saves a life, is it as though he had saved the entire world*".

Be especially respectful and attentive to the elderly. They have more life experience and knowledge than you and can be the source of some great advice. Besides, since talking doesn't come easy and may, in some cases, even be quite laborious, they tend to choose their words carefully (just like their selective hearing on the other end), so those they do utter, generally do carry at least some merit. And, sadly, you'll never know when is the last time you'll see them… Always keep in mind that you never know how much you will miss someone until they are gone.

Equally, if not more so, be especially nurturing and caring to the young; they are completely at your mercy and entirely yours to mold. The world needs responsible, righteous, contributing members, so PLEASE do your part in rearing good citizens for humanity's collective wellbeing. It's the right thing to do.

Speaking of the young, as they are the de facto future of humanity, we must address these little critters-Procreation in general (i.e., who should procreate, when they should endeavor to do so and why), what are our responsibilities; for having children in the first place, then as parents of course and the parental guidance and character building that just never seems to end (nor, unfortunately, is relegated to just our children).

I try to avoid allowing my personal emotions dictate what I scribe and to remain as objective as I can. I also do not believe in passing judgment, especially in blanket format.

Moreover, as I myself have been preaching, since every story is different and each person carries a unique set of emotional baggage; and every scenario is unique and every person reacts differently (due to the aforementioned emotional baggage, their level of intelligence, present state of mind, health, yada, yada, yada… this too was highlighted already), as long as people act within the law and abide by a somewhat palatable moral code, I try to avoid judging, criticizing people or even giving my opinion about what they say or do, but the subject of our children is quite different.

You see, rearing your children properly, cultivating them so they become responsible citizens who are contributing members of society and have a positive effect on humanity and is not some futile, pointless speech devoid of merit or logic. Children being the future of our species, they are of course of paramount importance, hence I devoted a section on this future of ours bit later.

Returning to corruption and inequality and where they lead their nations, just examine what happens in dystopian societies. Whether ruled by an absolute totalitarian dictatorship or an oppressive authoritarian regime; whether mired with corruption, cronyism, nepotism, rampant or cruel abuse of power and authority, or a combination thereof, the result is ALWAYS the same- Failure. Downfall is certain; what brings it about and when it ultimately occurs are the only variables.

Similar to my little tale about the erroneous notion of benefiting from networking with "aristocracy" (when socioeconomic status is defined strictly by one's financial standing, as is, unfortunately, most often the case these days), I often wondered why certain cities which are close in proximity, yet divided by a national border, have such different fates.

Why such close neighbors do not reach some level of equilibrium or "average out" in terms of quality of life, income, GDP and all other economic indicators. I live in Southern California. I have often wondered this about the two closest cities sharing a border- San Diego in the United States and Tijuana in Mexico.

San Diego ranks very high in terms of quality of life and the nation's habitability index. It enjoys beautiful weather almost year-round, a versatile landscape and rests by the meandering rugged shoreline Pacific Ocean, complete with lagoons and bayous. San Diego has many attractions, a formidable convention center, a recently revived vintage quarter and some history (insofar as California has "history" to begin with…), so the city enjoys a robust tourist industry.

On the contrary, Tijuana is, well… "anything but…". It is impoverished, seedy, caters to those seeking deep discounts on basic goods or cheap thrills. Of course it has its merits; some good institutions and, a lot more I suspect, inhabitants, but, overall, it leaves a lot to be desired.

The main reason for this glaring discrepancy is simple- Corruption. Whether a bribe being requested for a traffic infraction that never happened, staged accidents resulting in fake injuries, a robust narcotics and prostitution hub (to cater mostly to it's wealthier neighbors mind you) leading to all sorts of tourist trap schemes.

The same holds true for any other corrupt regime, ruthless dictatorship or any other purgatory-nation; the only question is for how long will they last and how many people will be tormented by these despots.

6 IDENTIFYING AND ASSESSING BUSINESS & INVESTMENT OPPORTUNITIES

As already discussed, but oh so important with everything else in life, the wise words of Reinhold Niebuhr "God grant me serenity to accept the things I cannot change, courage to change the things I can; and wisdom to know the difference" ring very true here.

So don't complain you have no access to the magic (but intrinsic volatility...) of high-frequency trading.

Or why about three dozen (of ever-changing, just like the boy-band Menudo) Goldman Sachs alumni run the world economy.

Or why Halliburton & Carlyle sign re-building/re-structuring contracts for regions where war has not been declared yet.

Or why the major film studios nourished a costly production environment that drove independent production away from its birthplace in Hollywood.

Or why the tobacco and sugar, among other major industries, did all they could to bury unfavorable studies regarding the harm their products cause. The sugar industry even went so far to fund studies which found fat to be the sole culprit and main cause of most heart diseases and diabetes when, in fact, both sugar and fat are equally culpable.

Or why some GMO ("Genetically Modified Organism") food producers systematically, sometimes even maliciously (and illegally) overtake natural crops with their own stronger & more viral genetically modified seeds.

Or why the pharmaceutical conglomerates created an insurmountable barrier of entry for FDA drug approval (and why their distributors do not get reprimanded for grossly violating the laws of narcotic medicinal distribution to questionable pain clinics (or, for that matter, most of the doctors who prescribe them). Yes, the same drugs causing the opioid epidemic. Up by a frightening 19% in the past year for which we have statistics, 2015-2016 alone, this terrible crisis took the lives of 64,000 Americans in 2016, costing over half a trillion dollars. By comparison, the number of deaths during the peak of the AIDS/H.I.V epidemic, in 1995, was 43,000.

Side note: To put the rapid rise of this catastrophe in context, compared to the aforementioned 64,000 deaths in 2015-2016, the number of fatalities in 1999 was 4,000 and in 2010 it was 16,000. Yes, a four-fold (400%) increase in six short years. Drug overdoses have become the leading cause of death for Americans under 50; with opiates accounting for two thirds of those mortalities.

What started this epidemic was the increased use of opioids, initially OxyContin and Percocet, to treat chronic pain. According to the Institute of Medicine, about 100 million American suffer from chronic pain (or believe they do; or pretend they do…). Prescribing opiates to "manage" pain is much more prevalent in the U.S. than elsewhere (about 300 million prescriptions, a $24 billion industry, in 2015… and growing), thus resulting in the U.S. consuming just about 80% of the global opiate supply. With certain opiates, like Hydrocodone, Americans consume 99% of the world supply. All of these statistics lead to one thing- This is purely and solely an American problem.

In a broader sense, in terms of overall drug abuse (whether illicit and prescription), the United States accounts for about 4% of the world's population, but roughly 27% (almost seven-fold, or 700%) of the world's drug overdose deaths. Quite a bit off topic, but so important, it compelled coverage.

Before returning to business and investment opportunities, just a couple of eye-opening statistics, provided by the non-profit organization, The Rules, related to wealth distribution to reflect on:

-The richest 1% of mankind account for 45% of all global wealth (the top 6% control 80% of the wealth).

-The 300 richest people on earth control approximately the same amount of capital as the poorest 4 billion people.

As unbelievable as it may sound, both of these are growing in disparity every year.

There is a monumental power shift unfolding between governments and corporate might around the world.

In terms of countries, according to the United Nations, there are currently 195 sovereign nations. Global empires have largely disintegrated over the

past two centuries. Towards the end of 1989, came
the fall of the Berlin Wall, to be followed by the
collapse of the Soviet Union just a couple of years
later. More recently, since the early 1990's, nations
too start tearing apart- Former Yugoslavia into their
pre-World War II republics of Bosnia & Herzegovina,
Croatia, Macedonia, Montenegro, Serbia and Slovenia
(with Serbia having Vojvodina and Kosovo as
autonomous provinces), Czechoslovakia into The
Czech Republic and Slovakia, and Eritrea seceded
from Ethiopia (the latter received it's independence
when the British withdrew in 1952). Palau also
became independent in the 90's and, since the turn of
the century, East Timor and South Sudan have
achieved sovereignty as well.

The self-immolation of a Tunisian street vendor,
Tarek el-Tayeb Mohamed Bouazizi, in December of
2010 eventually led to the Arab Spring of 2011 a few
months later (the first such civil disobedience to be
fueled and coordinated in large extent by social media,
by the way). Initially, these movements manifested
themselves in nationwide protests across Tunisia,
Egypt, Libya, Yemen and Syria with citizens
expressing their seething dissatisfaction with the
ruling regime at the time. In all cases, these
culminated in all-out civil war which led to a regime
change in most, while others are still in chaos.

In the summer of 2016, England opted out of the
U.K. in the now infamous Brexit vote; the full

consequences of which remain to be told. Since then, a wave of renewed fervor and increased separatist activity sprung across Europe; some in places which were festering for ages others brand new. The complete list includes no less than two dozen European nations. These are the more "outspoken" of the separatist movements- The Basque of both Spain and France, the Catalan of Spain, the Flemish of Belgium and, of course, the Northern Irish, Scottish, Welsh and even the Shetlanders (yes, there is such a group of people, no jokes please) of the United Kingdom.

Meanwhile, closer to the strife instigated by the Arab Spring are those brave fighters who ultimately defeated ISIS across Iraq and Syria, only to be deserted by their former "brothers-in-arms" without becoming their own sovereign nation, the Kurds.

I'm so sorry, I REALLY digressed here. As superfluous as the above may seem, it is important to know; trust me, Kurds are hot- My ex-wife is half Kurd… Needless to say, she is their self-proclaimed princess-in-exile. It is also important to review the above at a glance as "*we must learn our history so we do not repeat it*", as seems to be the case in so many instances; some of which are listed above. Simply put, for whatever reason, it seems our species just refuses to learn from its mistakes and change its course…

If our governments don't do this on a macro scale; it is up to us to do so on a micro scale. Whether it's global warming, violence in your neighborhood, a predator on the internet, a crime you can stop, or a person you can help make a better choice; learn from our past, get involved, take action and, in the words of Mahatma Gandhi, *"be the change you want to see in the world"*.

In terms of corporate power, Western societies generally shun the Japanese conglomerate model, that which is also prevalent with the largely family-run chaebols (Korean for "conglomerates") of South Korea, where just a handful of companies control the overwhelming majority of their respective economies.

Despite the West's aversion to the conglomerate model adopted by the Japanese and Korean economies and our somewhat trite anti-trust laws ("anti-trust" as in curbing (definitely not "preventing" because that never really took place) monopolies), companies have more and more power.

They are growing in market cap (a company's value given today's individual stock price multiplied by its number of outstanding shares) and the omnipresence of certain corporations, given the amount of metadata and information these companies have about us, is both daunting and much more than disturbing.

Given that, in just the two past decades, the three largest corporations in the world (yes, they are completely different) have grown sixfold in terms of sheer value while their labor force shrunk to about a tenth of the labor force. That means that the "capital contribution" of every employee in those enterprises is sixty times greater than it was a mere twenty years ago.

This naturally translates into those people who are employed by these behemoths being exceedingly wealthy and powerful. It equally means that, for every one of those same people, there are at least sixty people vying for their jobs, just waiting patiently for them to screw up. Whether by a slight oversight, a misstep, a deadline that wasn't met perhaps, a deficiency in corporate politics, sheer exhaustion and sexual misconduct; whether real or maliciously schemed (just because both DO happen, remember "Fatal Attraction"...? Of course you don't, so how about the more recent, and the more extreme example; here the villain fakes her own death, "Gone Girl").

I agree, enough. Back to the subject at hand. Difficult though it may be to overlook; perhaps not entirely "overlook"- You can still lament and vent all you want, but unless you are a U.S. or District Attorney, belong to a regulatory, enforcement or other governmental body with some level of authority on the matter at hand, there's not much else you can do, so don't waste any precious resources on impertinent matters or fruitless pursuits

If you practice that and focus on your goal without the unnecessary noise, jargon and drama that seem to afflict so much of our life.

There of course is no magic algorithm, potion or formula for success. Just as properly rearing children, producing an exceptional film or building a beautiful neighborhood; as the old African adage states, "*it takes a village*". Quite literally, for any of these feats to be successful, an army of talented, dedicated, loyal people who can work as a team is essential.

As for you, it takes all of the above, the ability to lead like a general (getting people to believe and follow you), the assertiveness of a salesman and the organization of an accountant. Beyond these you'll need to have a clear mind, an astute brain, a positive attitude, a strong work ethic, a determined (but open) drive and motivation, the ability to visualize, a keen eye (for identifying talent, potential opportunities and their probability of success, toxic employees or malicious partners, the challenges that lurk around the corner as well as long-term ones).

It requires the ability to identify, assess, sometimes even predict such "premonitions" as; forecasting economic cycles (in their numerous macro and micro levels), regulatory concerns and possible changes made to current laws and parameters, the competitive landscape, industry trends and the birth of new ones (conversely, the death of others), technological advancement, product life cycles, anticipating demand, estimating costs, pricing, production and delivery, time tables and, for many, assessing the political landscape, seeing what's missing where and finding a way to fill that void, finding a solution or more efficient way to accomplish a task, timing and dozens of other variables; both within and completely outside our control.

So, back to the task at hand- Identifying and assessing business and investment opportunities. These will be discussed in the forthcoming pages and, although there is no single algorithm for deciphering a source of wealth, there certainly are hints, characteristics, trends and certain parameters. We'll address these in terms of specific countries, industries, companies, societal needs, even individuals to follow.

I have always believed that, like with specific products/ goods and industries, if you "grow" with a country, you can make a windfall. My stepson returned to his grandmother's native China. Jonathan has been living in Shanghai for the past decade and is well-versed in both Mandarin and English. He is also well-educated, at least insofar as millennials go.

Having lived both stateside and in China for such a significant part of his life, he is well versed with both societies, their social norms and business cultures. Residing in the most dynamic commercial center of the most robust (by many measures, now the largest), economy on earth, can you imagine the different opportunities and potential for creating wealth inherent to such a place...?

Throughout history, rivers and oceans, providing the essence of life itself, became humanity's population hubs. Sustenance and nourishment in the form of water and food sources was plentiful. In these locales, commercial opportunities were diverse as both bodies of water provided the means for trade. To make trading viable and the city or town a major port or trading post, there was a need for an infrastructure to support the trading, shipbuilding, ground transportation, housing (and pubs and, yes, brothels). The better these businesses were, the more ships came to your port from the seas or stopped by you along the river.

By extension, terrestrial trading routes, such as the Silk Road (NOT Ross Ulbricht's, but the Han Dyansty's imperial envoy, Zhang Qian), it's ancestor, the Steppe Route as well as the Spice Route, Incense Route and the Trans-Saharan Trade Route were all similarly attractive for habitation.

By further "extension", the sprawling railroad labyrinth in the U.S., commencing with the Baltimore and Ohio Railroad chartered in 1828 rendered many isolated places accessible, thereby catalyzed the growth of existing towns and gave birth to many others. The railroads reached the frontier and the settlers followed almost simultaneously.

Side note: Despite their unwelcome annexation and imperialistic rule of India, when they finally left, in mid-August, 1947, following Mahatma Gandhi's devoted, yet noble, peaceful opposition, two of the most useful "gifts" they left behind was the establishment of a proper educational system and a railroad infrastructure unlike any other in the third world.

By the same logic, today's financial capitals offer the best opportunities as they attract the rich and the powerful who, in turn, need upscale residences, the very best appliances, furnishings and decor for those dwellings, luxury cars, fashion, jewelry and accessories, fine art, a myriad dining and entertainment options to appease every palate and taste and so forth- The very best goods and services money can buy. It is therefore no wonder that, generally speaking, the world's best museums, philharmonic orchestras, hotels, restaurants, luxury retail brands, designers, sporting teams and art galleries call Metropolis home.

But… We cannot all just bounce to New York to open a gallery or London to open a pub, so what do we do…? We look for the "up & coming" (the same term real estate agents use to describe a neighborhood that a tad less of appealing…). These are largely inexpensive, virgin markets that offer tremendous opportunities (provided you selected well, know the local culture so you won't get screwed and chose a stable place that isn't prone to violent revolt; or one that isn't likely to be leveled by a hurricane for that matter).

As with most of the industrial revolution, the years post World War II required a lot of human capital. War caused destruction; peace brought prosperity-Both meant increased production and expenditure.

The combination of the facilities built during WWII, coupled with technological advancements made in the same period (and largely for the same reason…), culminated in some monumental improvements in shipping methods and decreased delivery time. Some of betterment included the following- Sea shipping; larger ports (many a result of the war actually), canals which dramatically shortened many routes, bigger and more efficient cargo ships with more powerful engines, sturdier, better-designed containers fabricated from lighter metals and the use of cranes), better roads and upgraded overall infrastructure (remember President Roosevelt's "New Deal"…?), modern trucking and the dawn of air freight.

In aggregate, this meant we could transport goods globally in an efficient and cost-effective manner, so next was the need to find production centers with an inexpensive, yet reliable, work force. While I will save you the whole lineage of this exercise, I'll provide a basic timeline- Postwar Japan was the start, then came South Korea, Taiwan, Thailand, Brazil, Vietnam, India and so forth. As labor costs rose in one country, it's economy evolved to becoming a second world economy and, with the initial three countries listed, moved forward to join the first world and now (by "now" I mean the past few decades) represent some of the world's leading economic powers.

China was always a major contributor to this endeavor, but it's affect was limited for decades When China was still "closed" for international trade (it was never completely "closed", but trade was conducted through Hong Kong). Up to 75% of all imports and exports to and from China went through Victoria Harbor. Hong Kong, numbering no more than six million inhabitants during those fifty years; from the end of WWII until the British left in 1997, ending their colonial "lease", was "brokering" all these goods; BOTH ways, and enjoyed a windfall in the process. When the Chinese market "opened up", it virtually swallowed the globe's production needs. Today, only countries with an equal or lower per capita income can still compete- India, Bangladesh, Pakistan, etc.

Joining any of these societies at the onset of their trajectory would present tremendous opportunities and a chance for obtaining wealth; much more so then a stagnant or declining economy. And it matters not if you immigrated as an investor, chef, doctor, hotelier, car dealer, mechanical engineer, logistics expert or as a "bridge"; either sourcing products and services for foreign patrons, representing local manufacturers or a broker just buying and selling.

I remember visiting "The Billionaires Club" in Hong Kong- I could not believe how young some of its members were. After all, you just needed a good Rolodex (a "Rolodex" is a desktop card index used to record contact details, in the event you are a Millennial too…) which, if you were born into the right circle, was built for years before by your father. In fact, the wealth was so abundant that Victoria Peak atop the hills of Kowloon side across the harbor became one of the sot expensive neighborhoods in the world.

In the same vein, at the European front, it was also easy to decipher which countries would be the most notable emerging markets with the highest potential for wealth creation.

Commencing with Mikhail Gorbachov's "Perestroika" (the movement to reform and restructure the economy during the 80's), and, to a lesser degree, "Glasnost" (literally meaning "openness") until the dissolution Soviet Union in 1989, the Berlin Wall which came tumbling down (great song) and most of the Central and Eastern European countries, many ruled for decades with an iron fist locally and the Kremlin's watchful eye from afar, transforming from socialist or communist to market economies overnight, euphoric optimism and hope for a better future reigned across the continent.

Of course there were many countries involved in this monumental shift, so focusing on the most promising candidates would be prudent. These would be the gems- Those offering a solid labor force, know how in one or several manufacturing or service-related industries or attractive tourist destinations. Several examples of these are; Prague, the capital of the Czech Republic (formerly "Czechoslovakia") which, among it's many merits, is also a popular entertainment and cultural destination, Tallinn, Estonia's capital on the Baltic Sea, which became a high-tech mecca, or Dubrovnik, a tourist town in southern Croatia fronting the Adriatic Sea.

A simpler approach to trying and figuring out where, among the dozens of candidates spread across Central & Eastern Europe, you should invest your money or spend your time in, is to simply wait to see which country was (or is) about to join the European Union (the period I'm talking about started thirty years before Brexit, mind you, but extends to this day). EU membership did a few things- Initially, it guaranteed an influx of investment; both by member countries (and their wealthy citizens seeking diversification in these promising virgin markets) as well as local incentives, such as; an easing of credit standards, tax deferment among others. Either way, even after many suffered some set-backs initially, the standard of living rose in every such country which meant higher property values, rental incomes, etc.

Just these European countries, "re-joined" the world economy and became participating members of the global community (as is the case with China and Vietnam who have undergone similar transformations, as noted), the same would eventually take place in the former holiday heaven for Americans in the days Desi Arnaz, Cuba. Regardless of how one feels about the American embargo, Fidel Castro's atrocities and iron fist and all the bad blood as a result, one day Fidel would die (as he did) and slowly the inevitable will happen and Cuba will again open up to American tourism and investment (as it did).

Despite the ruthless regime and years of oppression, this beautiful island state and its warm, family-oriented, creative, intelligent & resilient citizenry persevered and are ready for the future. With its colorful architecture, cobblestone streets & nostalgic fleet of 1950's classic American automobiles, create the feeling of a "time capsule" like no other.

On top of this, the sensual salsa, the revival of pre-revolutionary Cuban music; son, bolero and danźon by world renowned ensembles, such as; "Buena Vista Social Club", inexpensive quality medical care which gave rise to a lucrative medical tourism industry, hearty dishes, such as; arroz con pollo, ropa vieja, boliche, even the American-born Cubano sandwich, savory sweets, such as; dulce de leche, flan and tres leches, among countless other options, the robust cafè Cubano, vivid tropical flora, exotic wildlife, endless sandy beaches kissed by warm turquoise Caribbean waters and, lastly, those delectable cigars we missed so damn much...Cohiba, Romeo y Julieta, Bolivar, Montecristo, Punch and Partagás make Cuba a highly attractive tourist, investment and retirement destination. That said, the biggest benefactors are those who came in when the U.S. embargo was still in effect; French and German concerns & wealthy investors from its neighboring countries, but you get the point; and it applies to different countries, cities or other locales, for a variety of other reasons.

Speaking of popular vacation spots from the U.S. and in the same region, here are a couple of other destinations; one that, by now, a mostly a missed opportunity in terms of investment and an "up & comer". First, Costa Rica, a favorite vacation spot for East Coasters, was an attractive investment opportunity until recently, when it became too pricey. So, just like with manufacturing, when the investment appeal of Costa Rica subsided due to rising costs, next in line will be Belize and, I suspect, Ecuador. Simple, you just need to get some facts, have some logic and presto! Deduce an answer or result to whatever you were pondering, which you will hopefully be able to identify and assess by doing your due diligence and research work.

As you can see, a lot of variables can make a place attractive for investment- A means and infrastructure for trading, a way to transport those goods, emerging markets, upcoming travel destinations, sources of inexpensive labor or know, etc., but there is more; a lot more...

Other historical examples of countries or regions that went from rags to riches in a short span of time are those places where resources which were high in demand at the time were discovered. I wrote "resources", although historically that largely meant natural resources, today it can also mean a human resource that is either very prevalent or can be obtained relatively inexpensively compared to other places.

Confusing...? Here's an example of each: When oil was unearthed in the Arabian Peninsula, it brought unimaginable riches to this region (whether you, as an outsider, could have benefited from that in this largely closed part of the world, especially back about eighty years ago, is a different matter altogether). In terms of human capital, the city of Bangalore (officially known as Bengaluru), is the capital of India's southern state of Karnataka and the center of India's high-tech industry. So, if you have ever needed some quality code written inexpensively, chances are this was the source.

At the onset of the industrial revolution, cities became interconnected, humans migrated en masse from rural areas to metropolitan centers and progress, in many forms, grew exponentially. From the first steam locomotives' usage of coal in the early 19th century, the need for various other natural resources grew with different inventions, their applications and uses and their facilitated transportation, a slew of Shangri-La's.

Just as oil made the Arabian Peninsula inordinately wealthy. This of course happened with the Arabian Peninsula, Iran and Russia in terms of sheer quantity; Norway and Brunei in per capita production and, on the home front, Alaska and Texas, both of whom are now undergoing a resurgence with fracking, though the low prices of oil, forced many U.S. oil fracking companies into financial demise. Following are similar accounts (although, because of the high demand for petrol (oil), the world's most traded commodity, most pale in comparison) of other origins of natural resources : Diamonds have brought riches (not to mention much strife and spilled blood) to Botswana and parts of Russia, Rubber, first found in Iquitos, Peru, and available only there for a thirty year period

(1880-1914) that gave rise to ruthless "rubber barons" who unleashed a reign of terror on the indigenous population. In fact, this is what happened in most of the natural resource rich lands in most of the undeveloped world and in countries who have limited personal liberties, are known for corruption or both. Last and perhaps the most familiar example of these is the California Gold Rush of 1848.

By sheer volume or variety of natural resources, some of the world's largest economies and most populous nations rank as the most plentiful (Russia, the U.S., China), but when pro-rating the list by population, a few smaller countries jump out- Norway, Brunei, Venezuela and the aforementioned Saudi Arabia, United Arab Emirates, Kuwait, Iraq, Oman, Yemen, Bahrain, Jordan and Qatar comprising the Arabian Peninsula in terms of oil production (the latter, Qatar, with a population of 2.7 million, also sits on approximately 15% of the world's natural gas reserves; talk about lucky…).

While natural resources and their transportation still bring about newly-created wealth (just think of the Baku-Tbilisi-Ceyhan pipeline, connecting the Caspian Sea to the Mediterranean through Azerbaijan, Georgia and Turkey), today's Meccas of growth in terms of resource include technological "braintrust" centers.

High-tech follows the same formula with Silicone Valley and it's neighboring San Francisco, New York, Los Angeles and Boston topping the list and three other U.S. cities (for a total of seven) in the top twenty. While the first four are very expensive, the barrier of entry to those cities is quite high. That said, other U.S. cities, such as; Chicago in seventh place (also quite expensive) Seattle in eighth (more moderately priced) and, especially, the relatively affordable Austin, (presently the fastest growing U.S. city), ranked fourteenth, all present opportunities for growth.

Side note: Not necessarily related to high-tech, here are a few other attractive U.S. cities poised for growth in the next decade or two. Each for a different reason, or combination of reasons, but all worth closer examination, if you're looking... Dallas, Salt Lake City, Ogden, Orlando, San Jose, Raleigh, Cape Coral, Denver, San Diego and so forth... So, just as I perhaps should have stayed in China many decades ago, or moved to any of the above-mentioned "returning" or "emerging" markets, you too should consider the benefits and the fit and perhaps move to a blossoming metropolitan center & grow with it.

Internationally, high-tech epicenters in the top 20 spots include Tel Aviv at fifth place, London at sixth and Singapore at tenth; all of which also have a high cost of living. That said, the Canadian cities ranked in the top twenty; Toronto at 17, Vancouver at 18 and Montreal at 20, as well as Berlin at 9 (arguably the new cultural capital of Europe since it was re-unified; unless the Fourth Reich rises of course...), are still moderately priced for being such major, modern and attractive cosmopolitan centers.

Calamities of all types and of differing severities & magnitudes also present investment opportunities. In these cases, you don't have to research nor guess; just follow the historical trends and the afflicted city's or region's median housing prices (relative to its cost of living) over the past two decades or so. Just make sure you have the financial stamina to withstand the storm, whatever it may be...

Back to potential investment opportunities... We all know "cash is king" and nowhere is that truer than during financial downturns. We mentioned the 2008 global economic collapse. As just one example Las Vegas Sands Corp. was the envy of Wall Street in 2007 with seemingly unlimited growth prospects in Macau where the company secured the most desirable parcels for resorts and sublet them to other operators while profit-sharing in casino revenues. Sheldon Adelson ranked as the third richest American with an estimated net worth of $28 billion. Following the crash, the company could not proceed with its development plans, suffered tremendous losses in its operating businesses and plummeted more than 90% in value; from its highest market cap (or, worth/value) of about $52 billion to just under $1 billion. Today, it's back at $53.5 billion... That's more than a 5,000% ROI ("Return on Investment") in less than a decade.

If stocks are not your "cup of tea", here is just one real estate example. Due to so many properties in Las Vegas being "upside down" (worth less than their outstanding loans, hence, even if they could keep their properties, many had no incentive to do so), tens of thousands housing units were up for sale; most often at less than the cost of building them… By now, many of those domiciles have tripled in value.

Remember the film "The Big Short" starring Brad Pitt, Steve Carell, Ryan Gosling and Christian Bale…? The latter portrayed Michael Lewis M.D. (yes, NOT a banker); author of the (very NON-FICTION) book this film was based on who was the first person to recognize the massive bubble in the American housing market which resulted in the above collapse; and bet $1.3 against it…

The city of Detroit, Michigan, declared bankruptcy on July 18, 2013. At an estimated $18 billion, it was the largest U.S. municipal bankruptcy in history. With this bankruptcy, an astounding 72,000 structures were abandoned. Today, while still mired with challenges, delays and set-backs, "Detroit Rising" isn't just a slogan, but a way of life; symbolizing perseverance, determination and commitment.

The bigger the calamity, the greater the fall; and potential for future resurgence (as a clean slate is easier to build on than one which needs to be demolished first), not to mention profit, of course.

I was in Manhattan just a few weeks after the horrific terrorist attacks of 9/11. As sad as it is to recount, not surprisingly, EVERYTHING plummeted in value and was offered for sale at pennies on the dollar across the city (remember how Damian Lewis' hedge-fund character of "Bobby Axelrod" got his initial significant windfall in the "Billions" TV series...?). At any rate, on that trip, I took note of a condo for sale- It was offered for sale at $120,000 by someone eager to leave the city behind; and quickly... I kept the address, just to check in from time to time. I recently checked that same property, and it was on the market again, for just under $3 million...

Places who suffered the wrath of Mother Nature (and will never be abandoned, thus required re-building) offer opportunity as well. A few examples where billions, actually tens of billions, would be required to reinstate normalcy, include the following; Hurricane Katrina ($160 billion) of 2005 bludgeoning Louisiana and Mississippi, Hurricane Sandy ($75billion) of 2012 slamming the Mid-Atlantic coast (mostly New York and New Jersey), and, more recently, in an unprecedented stretch of eight straight hurricanes between August 9 to September 29 of 2017, which included Hurricane Harvey ($200 billion) assaulting parts of Texas and Louisiana and Hurricane Maria ($90 billion) which pounced Puerto Rico.

Not the best alternative, but if you need a job, these places have much more available work than the local population could ever handle.

Other examples affecting an area's potential can be as seemingly insignificant as a company building a new facility. When that company is a world leader and the facility is significant, the resulting windfall, especially if the location is somewhat desolate or even just not right by a major metropolis. Such is the case with Tesla's Gigafactory 1 near the community of Clark, Nevada, or wherever the second Amazon headquarters will ultimately call home.

The above represent just a few examples. There are of course endless other specific reasons, or overall measures and parameters, leading to the growth of certain cities, locales or regions and how much, how quickly or when this bloom will occur. As with much else in life, timing is everything.

Insofar as growing or newly-emerging industries go, again, there is no formula, nor assurance, as to the opportunity each holds. That said, there are various trends, technological advancements & concerns and societal which need to be taken into account. With time; and some investigation & examination of the past, you'll be able to recognize trends, anticipate what's needed and where we're headed. This should shed light on at least some potentially lucrative business possibilities.

A few examples... As our population ages and people live longer, the geriatric industry; and associated goods and services, will inevitably grow. So... More need for (active, NOT dormant) communities and care homes for the elderly, nurses for both home care and these facilities, as well as walk-in bath tubs, stair lifts (as well as Viagra, Cialis and such...) and other essentials to cater to this segment of the population.

Climactic trends and changes also present their own opportunities. In even broad terms, the increase in natural disasters- Draughts (and consequential famines in some regions), hurricanes, fires, tornadoes have given tremendous rise in the market for survival gear, long term food rations and other emergency supplies for that upcoming Armageddon.

One eminent calamity is fresh water availability and the dire future of this vital commodity. This is a result of many factors and on-going phenomenon, most too intricate and complex to review here, but, if you're interested, you should watch the short films available through Green World Rising (on You Tube and many other places as they are distributed royalty-free, just to get the word out; very admirable). There is also a fantastic book I highly recommend: "Let There Be Water: Israel's Solution for a Water-Starved World" by Seth M. Siegel.

Obtaining water for human consumption involves its extraction water, the purification of water (by desalinating, boiling, distilling, filtering, Pasteurizing, iodine, chlorine/ bleaching and chemically treating the water; each to a different degree of purity) and its transportation. Another essential factor is of course water conservation. In terms of sustenance and to achieve self-sufficiency, irrigation with minimal wastage, is of paramount importance as well, but that's a whole different subject altogether.

Dean Kamen, the same brilliant mind we mentioned many pages ago who invented those push button Coke machines that offer a virtually endless array of beverage options, engineered a water purification system, SlingShot, but could not find a viable means of distribution for the refrigerator-sized machine to so many destinations, many of which are so remote they are virtually impossible to reach. By the way, the reason Mr. Kamen met with Coca Cola in the first place was to seek help distributing SlingShot after he got nowhere with governmental agencies, NGO's, even the United Nations; and of course Coke is the most widely distributed brand in the world, so where else…? His work and achievements are recounted in a documentary called "SlingShot" (yes- of course on Netflix…).

Water is becoming scarcer with each passing draught. 2016 was the hottest year on record. By 2050, it is believed that many places on earth will be incompatible for human life; the rising temperatures, lengthier summers, more frequent and wild fires. So it's not only water, but anything to do with cooling our continuously heating planet are potential goldmines and, it is fair to assume, growing industries.

Another looming catastrophe resulting from global warming is the rising water levels due to melting polar ice. Forget about what 95% of the scientists already concluded long ago, that starving, malnourished, gaunt, limping white polar bear from just before Christmas 2017 is testament to that phenomenon. Those rising oceans will submerge entire islands and obliterate the flatlands along coastal regions causing feculent stagnant bodies of water to filthy up our cities, attract disease-carrying mosquitos putting all of us under danger of malaria, yellow fever, dengue fever West Nile, Zika viruses and God knows what else.

As our energy needs grow and people are looking for green solutions to replace the depleting fossil fuel arsenal we have left at our disposal, renewable energy is a growing field (remember, as was the case throughout our evolution, "*Necessity is the mother of invention*"…), albeit with a lot of very questionable enterprises operating next to genius innovators.

We all know see the amount of jobs being lost to technological advancement; assembly-line jobs in factories cashiers' at fast food places, brick and mortar retail occupations of all types and, with the advent of self-driving cars, both drivers and mechanics, to name a few. A McKenzie Institute study completed in November, 2017, estimates that automation, some examples of which are mentioned herein, will cost 375 million jobs by 2030.

The past year will go down as the worst year on record for brick and mortar retail. More than 6,700 mass merchant stores across the United States will close by the end of 2017 according to the retail think-tank, Fung Global Retail & Technology. That will mark it as the worst year in terms of closings since 6,163 stores shut down during the financial meltdown of 2008.

In lieu of these, although more technical in nature (but that's where the human race is headed after all…), there is and will continue to be a growing need for coders, IT technicians, cyber security, people to oversee and manage your online reputation, among others.

A good place to gauge where we're headed, a good source of analyzing these trends are the individual books comprising the multi-Pulitzer prize-winning series, "The Oxford History of the United States".

Amazon does need a battalion of delivery people and Über and Lyft do need legions of drivers, but these will be short-lived; the first until drone delivery takes over and the second until self-driving vehicles will take over (do you ever notice how we are just being "taken over", step-by-step…?).

The alarming rise in obesity among adults; and relatively new phenomenon of child obesity, a terrible epidemic of dreadful proportions resulting in a tremendous increase in heart disease and stroke, high blood pressure, diabetes, certain cancers, gallbladder disease and gallstones, osteoarthritis and breathing-related diseases, including asthma and sleep apnea.

Personally exploring the dire health effects of a diet consisting only of McDonald's food for one month, Morgan Spurlock's 2004 feature documentary "Supersize Me" is both illuminating and infuriating. It provides an account of the multiple health risks and other forms of damage caused by such a diet in a period of just four short weeks.

On a related note, sleeping disorders affect almost as many people as weight problems (perceived OR real) but, unlike weight treatments, the ones for sleeping issues are relatively few and the competition not as fierce, for now... The weight control industry is huge and ranges from diet pills, to meals, support groups (also providing your sustenance on top of your social circle) workout machines and audiovisual programs for home (with related products) a million different diets (also with ancillary products, of course) and so very much more...

Sleep disorder treatments (other than a better diet and increased physical activity; a part of any prescription for almost all ailments) are quite limited. There are pills, though those that contain Melatonin are known to induce nightmares. There is the bedding we sleep on, but Mike Lindell and "My Pillow" pretty much cornered that market (not to mention the mattress market is tremendously competitive) and there are, of course, the CPAP machines, nose patches and surgeries specifically made for sufferers of sleep apnea. That leaves a lot of market to fill.

In essence, given technological advancements, societal changes, weather trends & natural disasters, social changes within your community, population variations and, of course, where you live, you can learn to anticipate, perhaps even predict, industry trends, societal needs and consumer tastes & preferences. With the amount of information readily available to us instantaneously, accomplishing this is not as daunting as may seem from first appearances.

Moreover, observing and evaluating the landscape (whether within an industry, for a specific product or within a geographical region) is also imperative. In doing so, you might identify something you saw in one place that you feel could work well or be popular, thus profitable, in another. Perhaps a void that you could fill or a need that is being underserved. These all offer opportunity, so keep your eyes and ears open...

That said, you must of course ascertain you're jumping on the train at the right station. Every new industry creates a cottage industry of enterprises; until technology catches up and until that particular market becomes significant enough for the big boys to join, bringing costs down, consolidating the industry and stream-lining both production and personnel.

An example of the first is personal- As a co-founder and the director of content for a high-tech start-up supplying content to mobile devices (before these could access the net). The learning curve of the industry and its regulation, the technology needed to create, adapt, host and serve this content to mobile devices while still being in business when the market matured enough to actually realize an income all needed to be perfectly synchronized. They were not.

Ever wonder why Home Depot dominates the home improvement retail sector when, only a few years back, it seems we had about half a dozen other merchants in the same space? Or why there are only Staples and Office Depot for stationary and office supplies? Or why Walmart, Target and K-mart are the only players left as general mass merchants? Or why the hell only Gillette manufactures advanced first-rate men's razors; and why are they sooooo damn expensive...? With the last example noted, Harry's, a discount mail order club for razors, saw an opening and need to fill...

At the onset of every industry; when it is still virgin and ripe, is when everyone jumps in wanting their piece of this freshly baked pie and the promises it holds. Believe it or not, early in their history, the U.S. automotive industry consisted of 3,000 car makers, today there are three (there are more, but the top three capture 98% of the market); actually, there are two as Chrysler is now owned by Fiat. The music/record industry followed the same exact path with almost 6,000 record producing companies at some point early down to a few dozen today (again, half a dozen of these dominate the market with a resounding 96%).

In the cases cited above, it is simply a part of an industry maturing; economies of scale- Both for cost-cutting measures and stream-lining production; as well as personnel and consolidation by mergers & acquisitions, resulting in an oligopoly at best, or even a monopoly...

There are countless other reasons for mergers and acquisitions, or consolidation, of course. Some boil down to remaining relevant in a changing marketplace- Other than it's incredible television holdings; channels, programming and both ancillary and tertiary businesses (and merchandising) Disney has built over the past three decades. To guarantee it's future and continued relevance (and dominance) it the market, beyond these brilliant diversifications, the company purchased three legendary entities and their properties; Lucasfilm (including Industrial Light & Magic, Lucasfilm Animation, Skywalker Sound Lucas Digital, and, most importantly for its longevity, the Star Wars film franchise and its merchandising rights), Pixar Animation Studios and Marvel Comics.

If you don't evolve (which is harder the larger, more "corporate" or older/ more traditional enterprises), nor diversify or remain relevant through mergers and acquisitions, you will perish. And it's usually a sad and gut-wrenching site. Just Google recent images of what has become from the once proud symbol of American ingenuity and industry from it's heyday as a sprawling and bustling Kodak complex in Rochester, New York, ever since the steady decline of film photography in the 90's.

I recall attending a meeting when Netflix just started mailing physical DVD's as it's original business model which was attended by Blockbuster executives (and international licensees and operators) in which Blockbuster did not even acknowledge the presence of Netflix, let alone the existential threat it posed in just a few years; given BOTH technological evolutions and advancements (which did require a leap of faith as will shortly be discussed) on top of a genius vision by Reed Hastings and Marc Randolph.

This coming year, Netflix is expected to create original programming at a staggering production budget of $8 billion (to put that in context, that is a higher figure than the estimated domestic theatrical box office revenues of ALL of the major film studios combined). At the same time, Blockbuster's remains survive only in vintage shops selling it's once gloriously illuminated acrylic signage.

In 1984, I saw the first "proper" coffee in Los Angeles. One that had flavorful coffee, a rich aroma, a welcoming staff, homely ambiance, dim lighting and newspapers scattered about (yes, it was a world without the internet. Despite why my children believe, there was such a time...). Knowing the popularity of such establishments "across the pond"; (no... NOT those in Amsterdam), but high tea in London, Paris' "Café Society", the cake shops of Vienna and just about any establishment selling anything in Italy, I knew Americans would discover the magic of coffee one day and, when they do, like everything in America, it will be BIG!

Yes, 1984 was indeed a good time to get into retail coffee; all you needed to make sure is that you were on the side of traffic heading to work in the morning.

By contrast, while the following represent great ideas from only a few years ago, today they have reached market saturation, to say the least (at least in my home town of Los Angeles)- Biergartens & Gastro Pubs, craft beer and cannabis cultivation (notice a particular "trend" in my research...? Good! I got something across...).

In terms of specific companies, this approach and type of investment is far riskier of course. There isn't much you can do once you've invested and you are, insofar as an investment in a single entity is concerned, putting all of your eggs in one basket.

Here it would be wise to follow a proven track record- Mr. Warren Buffet, history's best investor: Uncertainty is sure thing- Keep calm and carry on, diversify your portfolio, income is scarce so cast a net that can pay dividends and have a long-term approach to your investment plan.

As Mr. Buffet brilliantly summed up the above: "*Someone is sitting in the shade today because someone planted a tree a long time ago…*".

The above are Mr. Buffet's suggestions for an investment portfolio, but in terms of specific companies, he selects the undisputed leaders of their sector who dominate a market (Gillette, Coca Cola, Apple, Kraft Heinz, to name a few), never compromises on quality, assesses the difference between price and value, advocates and practices a long-term position philosophy, realizes that quality costs (but, at the same time, that same quality is often marked down in price, as was the case in the financial downturn described above), prefers to invest in those who have proven their worth rather than bet on the winning horse in an emerging industry, only takes advice from those he trusts and only invests in what he knows (hence, Berkshire Hathaway remained unscathed in the "dot-com" bubble at the turn of last century).

Putting these seemingly simple rules into practice and not swaying from them for just over half a century made this man the richest man on earth for the longest period of time in modern history. To quantify his success and put it in perspective, if you invested $10,000 with Berkshire Hathaway in 1964, that investment would be valued at $208,000,000, or over 1.9 million %, at the end of 2016. In terms of share cost, that would translate to $12.37 in '64 and over $244,000 at the end in '16. His own net worth

increased from $6,000 to $73 billion. Nice. No-
VERY nice.

Apple needed it's visionary founder back; both
YouTube and Netflix took a leap of faith that one day
technology would enable them to host and deliver
content in a seamless and personalized manner at a
high resolution; Amazon needed to surmount their
unfathomable physical goods delivery commitments
(first with endless human recruitment, soon to be
replaced with drone delivery), Facebook counted that
it's "exclusivity", at least initially, would obliterate
MySpace and Friendster (signs reading *"Cartago
Delenda Est"* (or,*"Carthage must be destroyed"*) adorned
the walls at Facebook- no wonder the latter two were
annihilated…); Google counted on crawling the
internet to harvest key words most comprehensively
thus spell the demise of Alta Vista, Netscape, Lycos,
HotBot, Excite and Ask Jeeves, among others.

And if you were there with them; and drank their
Kool-Aid, you made millions, perhaps more. All of
these titans obliterated their competitors and
dominate their respective markets (markets which did
not exist a few years ago, but are not only huge today;
they are essential). Moreover, each has ventured into
new territory far from their original scope of business
to identify, and conquer, the next "big thing",
diversifying into fields, such as; artificial intelligence,
augmented and virtual reality, self-driving vehicles,
space travel, crowd-sourced traffic mapping,

automated drone delivery, global mapping, social media, telephony, content manipulation, even producing hardware and goods as well as a physical newspaper and a brick & mortar supermarket chain… How very old school…

Other than countries and regions within them (or cities), specific industries or attractive companies to invest in; either by a stock purchase or actual active involvement in any place's commercial environment, one can also follow individuals- Either those they believe in; as had to be the case with any long-term investor in Apple, or those successful "serial entrepreneurs".

Needless to say, Warren Buffet ranks on top in both cases, but a few more legendary investors (covering the past few decades) include: John Templeton, Philip Fisher, Benjamin Graham, Peter Lynch, George Soros, Jack Bogle, Carl Ichan, Bill Ackman and Peter Thiel.

Needless to say, this is a sampling comprised of the world's top investors, some of which are no longer active. Secondly, of course you cannot invest in these people per se, but you usually can invest in their companies; most often umbrella investment groups or venture capital firms (sadly, all those life-altering opportunities from the people & companies featured on "Something Ventured" are long, long gone…).

That said, here are a few more names, courtesy of the
New York Times, that represent the most successful
venture capitalists and their firms, all of whom are
definitely worth further investigation/stalking-
Masayoshi Son (SoftBank), Bill Gurley & Peter
Fenton (Benchmark), Chris Sacca (Lowercase
Capital), Jeff Jordan (Anderseen Horowitz), Alfred
Lin & Neil Shen (Sequoia Capital; the latter from SC,
China), Brian Singerman (Founders Fund), Ravi
Mhatre (Lightspeed Venture Partners), Josh
Kopelman (First Round Capital), Steve Anderson
(Baseline Ventures), Fred Wilson (Union Square
Ventures), yada, yada, yada; you get the point…

Some of the above names also belong to the "serial
entrepreneur" list. These are folks that aren't happy
with one unicorn, or one home run, even a grand
slam- They made it before and plan on doing it again;
and again… Usually not for sheer greed or ego,
rather, because they really can and do make a
tremendous difference and, well yes, are also
concerned with their legacy. Some of the more
prominent and familiar names here include: Jay
Adelson, Rich Barton, Jack Dorsey, Shawn Fanning,
Janus Friis, David Heinmeier Hansson, Dave Hyatt,
Naveen Jain, Philippe Kahn, Justin Kan, Brad
Keywell, Eric Lefkofsky, William von Meister, Jordan
Mendelson, Matt Mickiewicz, Elon Musk, Yuval
Ofek, Ali Partovi, Michael Robertson, Peter Rojas,
Kevin P. Ryan, Joshua Schachter, Peter Thiel, Linus
Torvalds (though his biggest cost nothing; hence

make nothing, absolutely retarded…JK, great guy- A true mensch), Bhavin Turakhia and Evan Williams.

Needless to say, the above is a partial list and is NOT a ranking of wealth, corporate might or influence, rather, those who have founded MULTIPLE start-ups that were completely independent of one another and evolved into formidable & SUCCESSFUL enterprises.

7 FUTURE CONCERNS AND CHALLENGES

From a wider lens, just as the criminal world is not a good path to choose, even from a purely self-interest perspective and our innate and universal quest for longevity, procreation (and doing all can to produce upstanding offspring) is necessary for the preservation of humanity.

Just as with other looming catastrophes faced by our species; both in terms of ensuring it's continuity and that we have a planet to call home, we're not faring too well in confronting this challenge either.

At present, putting aside the longer life expectancy we enjoy and, in some places, immigration, almost all of the industrialized nations are hardly growing in numbers, are stagnant or even shrinking in population. Like all indicators, this one too varies from time to time so, while the estimates noted herein may not be exact, they do paint a very dire picture.

Japan is in the worst shape of all the major economies- its current population of 127 million citizens is expected to fall to 83 million by 2100. According to the Global Agenda Council on Aging Society as quoted by the World Economic Forum, precisely a third of Japanese are aged 60+, the highest percentage in the world. With people living longer and no one to fill their working shoes (or enough workers to sustain the aging populace), the ratio will inevitably worsen as will the economic forecast for the country.

By the way, the occasional threats voiced from time to time in U.S. elections about a looming 80% income tax, emanates from that same trend domestically. Though not as grave as in Japan, our future does not look all that promising either. The "Baby Boomers" represented the highest birthrate America has ever enjoyed. It was during the euphoric period following World War II when the nation's psyche was all promise and a time of tremendous economic growth. These were the children of the "The Greatest Generation".

When the "Baby Boomers" were society's breadwinners, the ratio of those working to retired folks was roughly 5 to 2. That means that 2.5 members of the workforce "supported", for lack of a better term, one retiree.

As the demographics shifted so drastically over the past few decades, we are not far from having that statistic inverted. That is, two workers will be supporting five retirees (God does indeed have a funny sense of humor- FML... Actually, FOL ("Fuck OUR Lives"...).

Sweden enjoyed a small "bump" in their population growth when the government gifted 150K Swedish Krona (equivalent to roughly $20K USD at the time) for every birth, essentially bribing couples to make babies. Beyond that, Sweden is one of the most socialist economies in Western Europe so the offer was even sweeter. But, as fate would have it, the combination of the growing aging sector of society and an influx of destitute immigrants, placed such a tremendous strain on the social security system, that its coffers and the support it provided the Swedes for so long, are now obsolete.

Not that the following is a proper indicator of any value, it is interesting to note that, at present, the leaders or heads of state, of Britain (or Great Britain, or The United Kingdom, or England- why does this country have so many damn names is truly beyond me...), Germany, France, Italy, Sweden, The Netherlands, Sweden and Luxembourg have NO children. In fact, of the major European economies, only the Prime Minister of Spain has kids; and only couple...

That said, we've all heard about our planet's population explosion. Recounting that tremendous growth, note that only 200 years ago there were less than one billion humans living on earth. Today, according to U.N. estimates, there are well over seven billion. Considered the most striking fact in this statistic is that today's population size is equivalent to an astounding 6.5% of all the total number of humans ever born.

For thousands of years, the population grew at a snail's pace, but, with the onset and advancement of industrialization, technological developments, medical breakthroughs and an overall society of better educated people that can contribute to solutions which improve global well-being, the pace of growth jumped dramatically. Between 1900 and 2000, that increase was about three times greater than during the entire previous history of humanity- From 1.5 billion to 6.1 billion (yes, in only 100 years…).

The projected population in 2050 is estimated at 9.5 billion and, in 2100, it is a whopping 11.2 billion. The only silver lining (see, there always is one…) is that the rate of growth has steadily been decreasing since the early 60's (after aforementioned The Greatest Generation was done having their Baby Boomers), but that unfortunately matters very little at the sheer quantity of bodies we need to sustain.

Side note: I love the word "but". It is the "great equalizer" of the English language.

So, overall, if rich countries aren't having babies, who is…?. By the way, I wrote "overall" as, even in rich countries, certain segments of the population have historically and will continue to grow in number. These include very traditional, at times secluded, religious communities, such as; conservative Catholics, devout Muslims and orthodox Jews. Outside of these communities, an aging population and, in some cases, immigration, the richest countries have the smallest level of population growth, at times, are stagnant.

In the United States, the Latino (a "catch-all" name for immigrants originating from Cuba, Central and South America) population is a good example of both. Though the net increase (immigration minus emigration) of this segment of the population has been decreasing over the past decade, in actual numbers, it has been growing rapidly. Initially, both immigration and a higher birthrate contributed to the increase of Latinos, but today only 34.4% of Latinos are immigrants (down from a peak of 40.1% in 2000) and those born here account for 65.6% of Latinos (compared to 59.9% in 2000).

Numbering 9.6 million in 1970, 22.6 million in 1990, they now (2016 statistic) number 57.5 million, accounting for 18% of the U.S. population; second only to non-Hispanic whites. Moreover, in just over two decades, one of every three newborns in the U.S. will be of Latin descent.

Side note: All monotheistic religions decree procreation as a duty and a virtuous deed- "... As for you, be fruitful and multiply; and increase upon the earth", Genesis 9:7 (the exact wording varies in different versions, but the message is identical). Likewise, most devout followers, largely irrespective of their religion, do not practice contraception. On top of all that, sinister religious leaders, as few as those are, mandate this edict to keep their populace improvised and helpless. In some places, to provide an everlasting cheap labor force; in others, to maintain an inventory of candidates for recruitment as mercenaries for violent acts of terror and uprisings.

Such is the philosophy of heinous rogue militias as the one depicted in the poignant film, "Beasts of No Nation", the equally troubling "Born Into Brothels" documenting the horrors (and consequences) of sex slaves in Kolkata, as it was true in the prevalent neighborhoods ISIS recruited from in European nations. The squalid districts of poor isolated immigrants at the outskirts of major cities.

The vast majority of these disillusioned adolescents are uneducated, destitute and hold bleak forecasts for their future- A very fertile recruitment community.

And not just for extremists- If you and a few friends
liquidate all your assets and head over to a poverty-
stricken province of a poor country, we could, in
theory build a private militia to serve in any battle,
real or imagined, of our choosing.

We cited some alarming facts and trends emanating
from the western industrial economies, or the 35-
member OECD countries, but what about the rest of
the world. Who is having these babies...?
Surprisingly, or perhaps not, Nigeria and Angola
boast the highest birthrate averaging close to seven
children per woman. Yes, countries with a per capita
income (annual income per person) of 800 USD and
3,000 USD respectively. Who follows these two
nations, you might ask...? According to the C.I.A.,
rounding off the top 20 are; Mali, Uganda, Zambia,
Burundi, Burkina Faso, Malawi, Somalia, Liberia,
Mozambique, Chad, South Sudan, Cameroon and
Guinea. In fact, the first rich modern nation to appear
in the list is ranked close to the 100 spot, some appear
around the 150+ spot, but most are at the very end of
the list.

So the highest birthrate is almost perfectly correlated
to the most destitute, underdeveloped countries with
the worst educational systems, poorest healthcare
institutions and weakest infrastructure. Very often
they lack even the basic necessities needed for
survival; clean water or electricity. Beyond these, but
to a far lesser extent, population growth originates

from the above-mentioned religious members of a variety of countries.

Bottom line, we need to get in the bedroom (or backseat of the car, or the beach (NOT recommended), or under the stars), get busy and make some babies! But we can't just have kids, can we...? These little critters are damn expensive-According to a recent study, about $250,000 to raise just one of them until the age of 18 in most of the western world. Today's growing income disparity is a major consideration of would-be parents; and rightfully so. For the record, that figure does NOT include private school, legal representation for delinquents nor wardrobes for fashionista teens.

As noted before, children require an endless array of character-building exercises, constant guidance for proper behavior, and trust me, more corrective behavioral measures (or "consequences"; today's politically-correct/ flavor-of-the-day term) and just as many educational, sporting, traveling, social interaction and cultural experiences as you can afford; both time-wise and pocket-wise.

They demand an inordinate amount of TLC, endless mentoring about redeeming values and the utilitarian benefits they bring about, the infinite and laborious process of instilling positive traits (what these constitute and why) and pointing that damn moral compass in the right direction. Rearing good citizens in the hope they become contributing members of society one day is an unbridled commitment, a daunting (sometimes, thankless…) task that never seems to end as well as a roll of the dice…

We do need to have more babies in the first world or we risk exasperating the already grave disparity in wealth distribution, having a far lesser educated, well off middle and upper class citizens and an exponentially larger segment of society that is impoverished, largely unhealthy and, unfortunately, poorly educated. Basically, fewer people who will, at least in part, need to care of a much greater (and growing) portion of earth's inhabitants.

If we are not proactive and procreate more, the looming capital and resource inequity, coupled with the increasing wrath of nature; more frequent and more extreme draughts (and consequential famines), hurricanes, fires, tornadoes, etc. and the catastrophic depletion rate of fossil fuels and, most importantly, water will bring us sheer havoc in the coming decades. *"The only Person who is more dangerous than the one who has all the money and power in the world, is one who has nothing to lose"*.

To illustrate the severity of the current situation, here is one example- The cost of fresh water in the third world. In third world countries, people pay up to 50-fold (yes, 5,000%) for fresh water than they do in the first world, spending up to 30% of their income to obtain just enough fresh water to survive. Mind you, this is not the gloomy futuristic picture painted above, but the case at this very moment. Can you imagine the mayhem that will ensue if the situation (i.e., availability and cost) worsens...?

Couple the water with the disturbing fact that the industrialized first world countries waste up to 40% of all the food they purchase (and about 25% of the food that is actually prepared or cooked) and we have a recipe for quite egregious social unrest in the not too distant future.

Back to us... PLEASE do your part to save the human race, keep it on the path of progress and help it prosper, but only if you are of sound mind of course, understand this undertaking fully, the responsibility it brings and commitment it entails. Last thing we need is another potential liability- We definitely need makers, not takers...

Side note: Back in my days as a producer and international licensing agent of content, I used to frequent the south of France quite a bit; Cannes, to be exact (not a bad gig, I admit). This was well before the introduction of that nameless derelict was forced into my life.

You see, I was in my late 20's/early 30's, making bank; both domestically by selling direct response videos (yes, people actually bought VHS cassettes through television ads...) and, internationally, as you already know, I had a knack for salesmanship which I entirely inherited from my father (he literally could sell ice to an eskimo, no shit), augmented by my relentless quest for knowledge concerning international political affairs which gave me a fair understanding of these countries, how to conduct business with them as well as their tastes and preferences, so I even had an idea what they'd like.

I was there ready to collect when the Asian Tiger economies took off throughout the 80's and when the Central and Eastern European nations opened up as a consequence of the Berlin Wall being brought down in 1989, the opportunities that ensued as nations went through their own revolutions one by one, culminating in the final collapse of the Soviet Union a couple of years later.

There was a lot of promise in the air, bags full of cash, and no set prices for these new markets, nor rules; just like the Wild West during the Gold Rush. And I was there at the doorstep of every nation, ready, willing and able. That said, I had to infiltrate, sell my content and capitalize on these opportunities quickly before they realized we weren't Warner Brothers exactly...

Anyhow, the point is I was young, making money and full of the appetite and enthusiasm young lads in that situation would be expected to have. I had an idea which was to purchase a chateaux in some beautiful village in the Provence region of France (they have a bunch of them and, in the 90's, when France wasn't doing all that well, you could have a sizable chateaux for a few million…), have children with 50 women of different origins and nationalities, but retain sole custody of the kids and raise them together. At the appropriate age, they would go to their mother's country of origin, but of course maintain close bonds within the family network.

Being that I would rear these fine specimens, my thinking was they'd obviously rise to the top in different spheres of life back home- Government, the military, the arts, technology, medicine, finance, banking, manufacturing, fashion, whatever… The point is that we would have a secret international network that is related by blood; even better than the Freemasons… But, alas, real life came a knockin'. So, I did try to contribute to the future of our species, but as my ancestors (and we) established long ago, "…*Mann tracht, un Gott lacht*" ("*man plans and God laughs*"). That said, I do have two beautiful children and did get a Chinese stepson; the latter of which at least proves I hedge my bets well…

It is unfortunate that so many parents do not
understand the gravity and importance of being a
parent. Larry Elder, the "Sage of South Central" and
host of his eponymous radio talk show, often cites
very disturbing statistics related to the most damaging
factor responsible for a failed childhood, leading to a
lost adulthood- The absence of a father. Check out
the Larry Elder website- Very informative and equally
shocking...

Illegitimacy (children born out of wedlock) resulting
in single-family households (almost uniformly, a
mother in that role), are one of America's most
damaging tragedies, in terms of our hopes for better
future at least.

Today, the overall illegitimacy rate in the United
States is 40.7%. Needless to say, single-family home
earn far less than two-parent households; about 40%.
Beyond that, the absence of the only parent in the
household, who is of course the only breadwinner,
hence usually at work, brings about further dangers,
potential harm and liability- Presently and in the
future. Devoid of the constant mentoring, guidance
and, of course, physical presence and all it entails,
more of these children are likely to suffer from
learning disorders, being a social misfit, able to curtail
violent tendencies and much more likely to join a
gang or otherwise descend into a life of crime
independently.

Such families are four times more likely to live in poverty. The children are twice as likely to drop out of school, twice as prone to conceive out of wedlock and three times more likely to be on welfare when they reach adulthood than the average American. In fact, the absence of a father, much more than race or socioeconomic status, is the leading factor in contributing to a criminal life.

The rate of illegitimacy is important because it greatly influences all statistical indicators of any population's progress or decline over time and, of course, it's effect on crime. Irrespective of race, 70% of all teenagers in correctional or reform institutions were raised in fatherless homes. That figure is almost identical to the percentage of most violent offenses (at any age) and the overall long-term adult prison inmate population.

So be a mensch and don't be a douche. If you have children; whether out of wedlock or while married (but then got a divorce), man up to your responsibilities, stand by your commitments, perform your obligations and do what's right.

Let the poignant words of one Frederick Douglass always remain in your mind: "*It's easier to build strong children, than repair broken men*".

They say *"good things come in small packages"* and, to
paraphrase John Burroughs, *"small gestures are preferred
to grand deeds"*. When I was a child, my father used to
put toothpaste on our toothbrushes. On cold
mornings, he would iron our school shirts so they
would warm us when we put them on. On those same
cold mornings, he'd warm up the car while we were
still in the house so it was comfortable when we got
into it. These were all symbolic gestures, but ones I'll
never forget and a kindness that reminded us just how
much he thought and cared about us. Everyday.

In the unlikely event you were wondering where the
notion of giving everything I do 110% attention and
effort originated from, observing these acts of
kindness was the source.

The opposite is that which is illustrated so eloquently
in the film franchise "Daddy's Home" where an
absentee father tries to make up for being MIA by
overcompensating and going overboard in trying to
conquer his children's hearts. What makes a
difference in a child's (or anyone's) life are those who
were with them through fire and ice, rain or sun, who
were present at every milestone, by their side fighting
through their ailments and helped them persevere the
hardships and overcome the challenges that life threw
in their path.

They say "*… the apple doesn't fall far from the tree.*" While that is not always the case, when it is, rest assured they (your offspring) will not be like you; they will be you 2.0; like you on steroids…

If you are an energetic person, your child will probably be a fireball. If you are lethargic, they will most likely be almost catatonic. If you are somewhat creative, your child should be a prodigy; if you are smart, they could be the next Einstein. As we evolve, as slow as that may be; our offspring's starting point becomes a bit more advanced than us. As technology evolves, as rapidly as it has in the past few decades, that foundation is moved substantially ahead.

No one really teaches us how to properly and effectively rear our children. There is no test to pass or license to procure (and renew). Every parent is afraid, every parent questions him or herself periodically and every parent inevitably fucks up from time to time. As long as the parent is of sound mind, mentally stable and their decisions are made with good intent, this is just a part of life.

Even though, there is a wonderfully witty quote on the matter by the astute Oscar Wilde, stating: "*Children begin by loving their parents; after time they judge them; rarely, if ever, do they forgive them*".

Your kids will teach you a lot (and VERY different...) things. In fact, if you keep your eyes and ears open probably more than anyone else in your life. Due to whatever circumstance or just because we were impartial at the moment, we all miss important life lessons. Our children present the perfect opportunity to rectify that- Better late than never...

Like the very simple (notice how so many things in life are just that- SIMPLE...?), very original and very true lessons presented in "All I really needed to know I learned in kindergarten" by Robert Fulghum. They are presented in very short essays that are ruminations on topics such as; holidays, relationships, surprises, empathy, honesty, death childhood and more.

The book strives to show how much better the world could be if adults adhered to the same basic principles and code of conduct we teach our children in kindergarten; i.e., sharing, caring for one another, cleaning up after ourselves, being considerate, how to properly interact with one another and how to live a balanced life consisting of work, play and learning.

Just as with life lessons, your kids will also give you another chance to have a "second childhood"; enjoying those things you have a child once again and experiencing those which you never had before. Just as a new puppy brings life to an aging, lethargic dog, so will your kids to you- Animated films, laser tag, mini-golf, paint ball, foosball, air hockey, bowling, sports of every kind and video games you never fathomed would ever exist. Oh, and HOMEWORK! In short, they will enable you to re-live your youth in today's world; quite different than when you grew up, irrespective of when that was.

They will also provide you with one of the few, and probably most significant, ways to achieve one of life's most important goals for many- A testament to who you were and the preservation of your legacy, perhaps even a continuation of it. If a little vanity helps mankind, so be it...

There is of course an inordinate amount of thoughts, suggestions and information on the topic of children, but this of course isn't the place to delve into those. That said, as this subject is of paramount importance, even essential for the survival of mankind, I am presenting what I hope are some engaging ideas and vital points to ponder, especially those faced by today's "i Generation" and, us, their parents.

First, again, to put things in perspective; and acknowledge that, as a race, perhaps we're not as evolved as we like to belief... Education. The modern K-12 educational system we all know today as the norm is only about 150 years old. It was first introduced by Horace Mann with the establishment of the first statewide educational system in Massachusetts in 1852, extended to all states by 1918.

Being that young and since we all know that there is no "one size fits all" with anything in life, the system is still evolving constantly and undergoing consistent adaptation to accommodate for differences, such as technological advancements, a particular community's unique needs, socioeconomic factors, cultural differences, budgetary constraints, living environments and so much more…

Keeping the young age of this institution and all the factors requiring consideration, the appropriate amount of homework (if any…), tests administered (if any…), even the proper amount of hours (and when) kids should be in school, are all under constant debate.

Just as one example, we've all heard of the strict parenting and often excessive amount of hours certain societies demand from their children. Whether in the book "Battle Hymn of the Tiger Mom" or the illegal late night tutoring and study halls hidden across South Korea (no shit…). In fact, this approach has become the cornerstone of education across most advanced Asian nations.

On quite the opposite end of the spectrum are societies that are much more lax with their children's schooling and put a bigger emphasis on social interactions, public responsibility, nature & the great outdoors and a lot more elective classes that foster individual choice and habits that cultivate independent thought. This naturally takes time away from "formal" education, so much so that, in certain segments of societies, Finland for example, there is no homework, there are no tests and students spend less time in school.

Which school of thought fared better, you may ask...? Although completely contradictory in both their beliefs and their approach, the aptitude of the students and testing results (or "ranking") are surprisingly almost identical.

One of the aspects of our children's education that is no longer under dispute following the correlated results of many studies, is at what time should school start every day. Almost all findings point to around 9:30 AM. So, let me ask you- How many K-12 schools do you know who start the day at that time...?

Whichever way you choose, give it considerable and remember, as Nelson Mandela expressed it so perfectly, *"Education is the most powerful weapon in which you can change the world"*.

In terms of individual treatment, a customized approach and recognizing the best fit, the subject of education is similar to both legal representation and medical treatment. Many times it is you who knows which choice or course of action "feels" right. After all, regardless which of the above a decision relates to, you are the one who has spent the most amount of time thinking and evaluating the available options and, in both cases, you and your family have the most to lose; whether the decision at hand is educational, medical or legal decisions and whether it will directly affect your children or you. If it doesn't "feel" absolutely right, question it. Study the issue, investigate and weigh the options, then decide. It is you, and your child, who know what's best for him/her.

In terms of educational options, this line of thinking is the primary reason for the rise in both homeschooling and charter schools popping up everywhere in recent years by the way.

We are all aware of the dangers and potential traps of the internet. Those mentioned at the very beginning of our journey. Again, this isn't the place to go into further detail about the perils of the internet- You must be proactive in seeking the answers and how to best safeguard you and your family from this potential monster.

What I would like to present for discussion are the consequences of our, and more so our children's, gross overuse of all the net has to offer and means by which we connect to it; i.e., our "screen time".

Some of the dire consequences of this screen addiction are common knowledge- We are well under way to reaching the global population's halfway mark of those who own a smart phone. Almost without exception, all have and continue to suffer tremendous damage to their social life; both in terms of their ability to connect with others as well as the quality of those interactions. The same number of people, to one degree or another, are victims of a decline in their capacity to concentrate and to remain focused as well as in their cognitive abilities overall.

In short, almost 2.5 billion people with ADD at present and, according to Statista, an estimated 5 billion smart phone owners, hence, ADD sufferers, by 2020.

Not surprisingly, the number of adults diagnosed with "ADD" ("Attention Deficit Disorder") and its neurodevelopmental counterpart affecting children and adolescents "AD/HD" ("Attention Deficit Hyperactivity Disorder"), have skyrocketed in recent years. These diseases are characterized by problems paying attention, excessive activity, difficulty controlling in appropriate behavior.

These symptoms of course lead to a Pandora's Box of related harmful effects stemming from an inability to get an adequate education, or to behave appropriately in social situations, be attentive and concentrate. The resulting anxiety, angst, low self-esteem, even rage, as well as other mental damage and emotional toll these inflict go far beyond the initial detriment to one's wellbeing.

Even if not afflicted with AD/HD, the entire "i Generation" is in peril. While studies vary, it is estimated that these kids spend anywhere from 7 to 9 hours a day in front of a screen. Today's teens report a 57% increase in sleep problems in just the past 25 years ago. Teens need 9 hours of sleep each night; less than 7 impedes their growth, thus is dangerous not only to their development, but also their ability to concentrate (and be responsive) at school.

The culprit isn't only our mobile device. The threshold for excitement and the level of stimuli needed to keep children engaged, has tremendously changed as well- Just compare the original "Jumanji" film from 1995 and the one released in 2017. They're like night and day, literally.

Sleep is absolutely necessary for to retain a healthy memory, proper metabolism and, as we all know all too well, a good mood. This of course is universally true for every living human being (except for me) regardless of age, race or gender.

Side note: Do NOT let your children (or you, for that matter) sleep with your mobile device or PDA; in fact, they should be at least 10 feet away from them/ you at night. The blue light emitted from these devices affects your EMS ("Electro Magnetic Field") which then manipulates your circadian rhythm to think it's daytime and hinders, even completely stops, the production of melatonin which affects your sleep extremely adversely. The best thing to do is just keep them all in one "charging area", like the kitchen. That way, you're also sure your kids aren't playing or on social media until 4AM.

The social ramifications are virtually endless... A successful post; one acknowledged by many "likes" or "re-Tweets", releases dopamine which cause us a euphoric feeling quick fix. Just as other addictions work, once that feeling of pleasure is gone, it needs quick replenishment. Yes, this works just like gambling, alcoholism, drug abuse and all other forms of dependencies and addictions. And, to think, in my day, "viral" only meant one thing- Diseases. There was nothing good about that damn word, but today...

Conversely, the aggregate harm to one's ego, confidence level and self-esteem caused by a disappointing response, or "unsuccessful" post is scathing- It is an agonizing and penetrating pain our children feel almost on a daily basis.

And all the damaged calamities described herein of course exclude actual malicious online schemes and cybercrimes, as described above, such as; cyberbullying, cyberstalking, catfishing and it's many nefarious uses, exclusion, impersonation, outing, trickery, denigration, flaming, disinformation, misinformation, shaming and trolls- It's like fucking Disneyland…

In the event you needed some additional alarming facts and figures resulting from the aggregate effects of the above, please note the following:

In the period since the introduction of the first i Phone in 2007 until 2013, the amount of teens who said they feel "rejected" increased by 36% (that is within a 6-year period).

Playdates have decreased by 40% between the years of 2000 and 2015 (and, if we're being honest, many of the playdates result in social screen time, peer or competitive video or online gaming).

Beyond all of the above, there is the very obvious sexual predatory dangers of the internet. These can range from an adult pretending to be a child or teenager and trying to coax minors to engage in texting, virtual sex or of even a physical encounter leading to molestation, rape or even abduction.

Have as many safeguards in place as possible; and all your kids' passwords in case something happens to them and so that you can monitor who befriends or tries to reach out to them, etc. (of course, you should do this to a certain degree and age; to which age and to what degree you need to figure out between yourselves). Using the internet requires a certain level of maturity and your kids must understand that, despite what they may believe, there are child molesters, pedophiles and other deranged sexual predators that are deceitful and devious, far beyond either of you can imagine.

Think about it (and, try at least, to explain the same to your kids) - Would you sit at a park bench watching your kids play in the park right in front of you and allow one of them to simply leave without asking or even telling you where they're going, cross a busy street and play elsewhere out of your field of vision and sound. That's the analogy for children of course; as the offspring age, they differ, but the idea remains the same.

Case in point: I was talking to a friend of mine about this topic, specifically physical meetings culminating in sexual assault, rape or abduction. She said her children know to beware of strangers; just as they are in real life. To that I said that's great, but these predators know how to lurk, collect info, pretend to be someone the kids know (or a friend of someone they know); it is far easier than you think, then befriend them for a period of time; finally luring them to meet. You see, at that point, they are NOT meeting a stranger...

Just remember, the amount of information that is available on you on the internet (of course it varies greatly between what is available publicly and privately) is vast and plentiful. It is imperative you are very selective with whom you share information and limit it as much as you can whenever possible.

Other than the social, physical and mental implications described above, there has been a significant decrease in feeling independent, being safe and, of course, a part of the blame in the alarming increase in child obesity can also be traced back to the inactivity caused by those screens we all adore so very much.

With gaming, every parent faces similar issues with regards to their ratings- The young ones want to play Teen-rated games while the teens want to play Mature-rated games. Whatever they tell you, just keep in mind that first-person shooting games were initially developed for military training purposes- NOT to practice shooting or aiming, rather, to desensitize soldiers in shooting their fellow man. Now, how many parents know that tidbit of information…? I'm not saying that is a bad reason to develop these games for training Marines going into battle, mind you; I am however saying it might not be the best thing to babysit your eight year-old…

This is an ongoing battle and, yes, your children will say all their friends play a specific game (just like they'll say all their friends have Snapchat, or Musically, or whatever…) and that you're ruining their only chance at social acceptance. Also worth noting is that, however hard you try, just recognize and accept the fact you'll never get ahead of your children with technology- It's an ever-changing vortex and quite simply because they decide what's hip, hence what survives.

The above will be one of the first, but many, social acceptance-based peer pressure situations you and your children will need to address, compromise on and overcome. As such, don't take it in stride and find a way to resolve them in a manner that will work not only in this instance, but consistently with upcoming situations. Don't worry…These future challenges not only include the never-ending educational/ studying battle, but also a (very…) fluid sleeping schedule, alcohol consumption, drug use, sexual activity, in many cases also tattoos, piercing and other flesh-mutilating expressions of art… FUN!

These phenomenon will all unfold almost simultaneously the to the most overwhelming period of your children's lives commencing with your children undergoing puberty; and their physical appearance completely changing, not to mention their emotions toyed with by hormones. Concurrently, they will face tremendous social challenges (in multiple facets- cliques, sports, attire, after-school activity, school dances and other social engagements) not to mention their first love, first heartbreak, then the second, the third... And, towards the middle of high school, the pressures of what looms ahead and what to do with their future- College, university, a vocational institute, the military, hit the job market, or even a year of volunteering in a form of social service; and the challenges each one of these choices presents. EVEN MORE FUN!

Whatever you do and however you handle it; be calm, be patient, be understanding, be empathetic and understand that, no matter what you do and how hard you try, it will not be a smooth ride. Understanding the complexities and accepting that it will be a tough journey from the onset, will make the journey more palatable and help you and your children come out the other end relatively unscathed with your relationship intact. If that's the case, it'll be stronger than ever.

The same screen addiction resulting from gaming and social media are also responsible for the decrease in socialization we broached a few times already; both in interpersonal communication and interaction. In the 80's I remember comparing the East Coast and West Coast along the same lines. People back East used public transport much more, they generally encountered each other in elevators if working in the city and lived in more densely packed urban centers more often. By contrast, in the West, traffic was getting a lot worse and people hardly used public transport and, for the most part, lived in suburbia keeping them away from one another more and more as the years passed and limiting their interaction with others.

Today, with social media, dating sites, online shopping and video/ mobile gaming, the interaction of both children with one another and adults alike has created an environment where impersonal interaction is virtually nil. This of course has tremendous ramifications in every facet of life, the overwhelming majority of which are negative, in some cases, even detrimental.

On that note, we all know that child obesity and its direct impact and immediate contribution to the increase of diabetes (currently afflicting about 400 million people; and counting…) and a similar rise in heart disease and heart failure.

According to the American Heart Association, for 6-11 year old children, the prevalence of obesity increased from 4% in the early 1970's to over 18% in 2010. That is a mind-boggling increase of 450% in 30 years.

The prevalence of overweight in adolescents ages 12-19 increased from 6.1% to 18.4% in the same period. Seemingly not as bad, but still a whopping +300%.

While genetic and environmental factors (not surprisingly, lower income households are more prone to obesity) play a part, the Center for Disease Control and Prevention cited "caloric imbalance" as the main culprit; i.e. our children are eating more calories than they're spending. Other than the above, the main culprits for this imbalance are inactivity of this generation and the contents (namely, fat and sugar) as well as the super-sizing of everything they shove in their mouths.

While the initial incarnation of "Super Sizing", first introduced by McDonald's in 1992 until being terminated in 2004, is gone, the concept caught on. From Big Gulps that can only be lifted by Marines fresh out of bootcamp, to burgers stacked so tall only a horse can fit them its muzzle and deep-fried butter (no shit- please do look that one up...), the culinary genius of contemporary times seems bent on ending the human race, one way or the other.

By 2012, more than one third of children and adolescents had a weight problem with the epidemic growing in severity every year.

Drug abuse is of course another societal epidemic affecting our future outlook and it too is quite grim, especially when considering that, like obesity, it is adversely affecting both our present and our future. While not reviewing the decades-long crystal meth literally melting the Heartland, we've skimmed the highlights of the opiate epidemic with adults. Here is where we are with our children...

First, the introduction of narcotics to our children so easily and so early in life is detrimental. The quick fix shot-gun approach our health care system. According to the CDC, the percentage of children ever diagnosed with ADHD grew by a frightening 42% between 2003 and 2011; from 7.8% to 11% of the U.S. population ages 4-17. By 2011, 3.5 million children were taking medication for ADHD, one million more than just eight years prior.

As one example of the continuing disturbing trend of the above, using Adderall (often prescribed to treat ADHD) as a Litmus Test, it's use among high school seniors has increased by 39% in the seven-year period between 2009 and 2016.

According to the non-profit organization, Do Something, not surprisingly, more kids die from prescription drugs than heroin and cocaine combined. And equally not surprising is that 60% of teens who use prescription drugs get them from friends and relatives; for free nonetheless...

By eighth grade, 28% of adolescents consumed alcohol, 15% have smoked cigarettes and 16.5% have used marijuana. Four years later, by their senior year, 22.7% smoked pot in the last month compared to 16.3% who smoked cigarettes in the same period.

The most promising statistic in this grave area of concern...? Teens who consistently learn about the risks of drugs from their parents are about 50% less likely to use drugs compared to those who do not. Something to ponder... The same is true for the next topic of discussion- Teen pregnancy.

One in three American teens will become pregnant at least once before the age of 20- That's nearly 750,000 pregnancies each year, an estimated 25% of which end in abortion. About a quarter of teen moms have a second child within 24 months of their first baby.

Teen parenthood is the leading cause of girls dropping out of school; less than 2% of teen moms earn a college degree by age 30. Teen pregnancy is the most certain path a girl can pave to poverty; a full two thirds will be relegated to a life of destitution.

The silver lining here (we must always have one, or else we're doomed, right...?)- A more open attitude and candor discussion; both at home and in schools (and better knowledge and educational tools to conduct this discussion with...) as well as the much more prevalent use of contraceptives, has led to the teen pregnancies in recent years to be the lowest it has been in 70 years! In fact, the lowest level ever since teen pregnancies have been tracked way back in the 1940's...

What much of the above clearly illustrates and teaches us is that we can, should and do make a difference. Once more, just like a Marine- Ready, Willing and Able. So, please try to avoid self-pity and possessing a victim mentality- These provide no benefit and get you nowhere. Try to let go of taboos, so your can open up and so that your children feel comfortable talking with you about such significant issues. Doing so may prevent a life of misery; not doing so could be catastrophic and cause damage you will not be able to undo.

Don't degrade yourself and your family to the notion that it's the government's fault, or the shortcoming of the educational system, or the graphic violence and gratuitous sex of video games and films, or the hours spent in front of one screen or another frivolously interacting on social networks or engaged in endless searches for video clips and related stimuli, nor even the moral compass prescribed by those celebrities our children are so addicted to in reality shows or follow on social media.

As Ralph Waldo Emerson noted over 150 years ago: "What lies behind you and what lies in front of you, pales in comparison to what lies within you." Truer words were never spoken.

I want to express my gratitude to those who have helped me write this book- My dear friends, Josh Arieli and Spencer van Houten. My other dear friends who proofed it- Joel Bailey, James Chien and Jonathan Peng (a lot of Asians in my life, I know...) ... And I want to thank 3M for the, albeit accidental, invention of Post-It's without whom this book would have been a far more daunting challenge to accomplish.

And, of course, I want to thank you for the interest and support; I hope you feel enriched in some way and more positive, or at least more optimistic for the future that lies ahead.

I am no Polaris, but I do hope you enjoyed our journey together and do sincerely wish you find your peace, harmony and your way home.

Live well, be good and prosper.

Love,

Tal.

PROLOUGE

In today's digital age, information is readily obtainable within seconds. No matter the topic, no matter when, where or whom; and we don't even have to type our desired search, just talk into our phone.

This is a far cry from when I was growing up (which wasn't that long ago), but in terms of research methodology and tools available, I might as well have lived in the dark ages.

As a kid, I remember walking down to the library to do any research. Best case scenario, they had Microfiche to look through, but during most of my early years, I went through index cards; many of which were illegible, others torn or otherwise damaged and some missing altogether. If the universe was in balance and the gods were smiling, I'd even be able to find the book I was interested in, but that was seldom the case of course. As such, the best I could ever hope for was having one source of information, written by a single person from his/her own narrative without the ability to augment that information, question it in anyway nor investigate other records.

Very, very different than the immediate gratification of present day. Anything you want to learn about, explore or investigate is unveiled in words, images or video within seconds. Yet despite this instantaneous access, universal to almost all matters one could ever wish to learn about, it appears that our society has diminished in its intelligence, rather than expand people's horizons and enrich their lives.

I believe this is the culmination of many things. One of which is our collective (and growing) ADD as a species, another is our disinterest in matters that do not (or seemingly do not) concern us in the immediate future and, quite simply, due to the overwhelming amount of information we are inundated with on a consistent basis.

I forget what the exact comparison is (and it grows in polarity every year), but it has been noted that today mankind writes about as much information in one month than we did since the advent of scribing until around the 1950's, in aggregate. The same thing can be said (even to a more extreme extent) about music, and, of course, video/film content (as the latter did not exist until recent history and only much later available for people to create such content personally; first with heavy, cumbersome, bulky and expensive video cameras just a few decades ago, evolving rapidly to much cheaper handheld consumer cams and, just a few years ago, through a device we now almost all

own and have with us at all times; the smart phone).
Isn't the exponential progress of evolution mind
boggling…?

Just this very moment I spoke with my son about
how The Godfather film couldn't find a home with
any film studio for years until being made, only to
realize he didn't know what a film studio is… or a
VHS cassette, or an audio cassette, or a micro cassette
recorder. All common devices which were used in
multiple aspects of our lives, not to mention invented
not all that long ago. They, like much more in our
lives, have come and are forever gone. In many ways,
akin to Julius Caesar's "*Veni, vidi, vici*" ("*I came, I saw,
I conquered*").

All was dandy until about a decade ago at which point
I endured a very tumultuous divorce (is there any
other type…?) and had a toxic business partner
unwillingly introduced into my life; and in every
business enterprise I had a stake in. Together, these
challenges drained my energy, ravaged my soul,
consumed every moment of my time and brought my
life's journey to a halt.

You see, resources are finite. Such is the concept of
"Opportunity Cost"- doing one thing is always at the
cost (or opportunity) of doing another. This includes

monetary consideration, time, energy, work, or any other tangible object or scarce resource; just as theorized in the Newton's third law of physics.

There is a silver lining in everything, isn't there...? and "what doesn't kill you only makes you stronger", right..? My silver lining is growth, the apex of which will unfold in the pages to come. My hope is that you find some value, a little recognition, an understanding and put into practice that which you deem worthwhile from the ideas set forth.

Look at the half of the glass that is full. Recognize and appreciate what you have; as noted before, do not waste time on what you do not have or those you think have more. The "neighbor's lawn is always greener" is seldom the case; and, if it is, there's not much you do about it, so, again, focus and expend the resources you have on you and your goal, ONLY.

All writers, directors, actors, talk show hosts and stand-up comics, just as those professionals listed above are merely storytellers. Each has his/ her own narrative, field of expertise and information that can, and should, be harvested by all of us and serve to benefit us all.

Just the same, though not nearly of the same pedigree like my father, and his father before him, I too believe

I am a story teller (or, at the very least, have something to say…), hence I gathered and now I wish to unveil and to share with you that which I have learned.

As it is said in John; Chapter 9 Verse 25: "…one thing I do know; whereas I was blind, now I can see." Worry not- I am far from being a religious scholar, nor even practitioner. That said, as I endeavor to do with all that I encounter in life, here too I wish to extract what value I can. Worry not, this undoubtedly is my Magnum Opus, my "swan song" as, clearly, I am far from being a writer.

There are however two instances in which this would happen- If I realize there is more I have observed or experienced that is worthwhile to share and ask people to sacrifice their time to read and I, in hindsight (which we all know is 20/20), I realize I misspoke or made a mistake along the way. Being a mature adult warrants self-examination. As noted, if we're not honest, evolved or humble enough to stand in front of the mirror, at least look at it when someone else holds it up for us.

One of the traits that I most admire in people is the ability to admit an oversight, shortcoming or mistake; as small or grand as it may be. This humility essentially means one does not think he "knows it all" and is open for both discussion and to learn.

This is why, when Bill Gates made revisions to some of the notions outlined in his monumental book "The Road Ahead", I was aghast. What a mensch! A man of his stature and intelligence to realize, publicly admit and correct that which he feels was erroneous in his initial thoughts, is tremendously admirable. Besides, now we know he really is human...

Timing is everything. Ask a child to eat, drink, watch, read, do or otherwise be engaged, participate or experience anything prematurely and the results can be catastrophic, even lethal.

From my perspective, I feel the time is right for this manifesto because, at the tender age of 48, I was recently diagnosed with diabetes, an ensuing neuropathy condition and suffer from severe sleep apnea for years. I am also a member of the fastest rising mortality group, largely attributed to the combined symptomatic trifecta of blood pressure, sugar level and heart condition.

From "your" end, I am afraid mankind is descending into an abyss of morass and that soon most human cavities will be encapsulated in a cocoon at a catatonic state; frozen both in time and place akin to a state of comatose. Perhaps suspended in a hive and connected to a network of electrodes that will enable sensory manipulation and the intake of sight, sound, smell, taste and touch. Perhaps, at a more evolved stage, even that of feeling, mood, thought and consciousness itself.

After all, the virtual reality simulators already in place allow us to experience a flight, perform a surgery or travel to any destination as if it were real. So why strive for wealth, what motivation is there to learn anything, why bother to study a vocation or what incentive is there to even work if we can obtain any information we seek immediately and get into a simulated environment of altered states and actually feel as if we're embedded within a pride of lions in the Serengeti, living the high life in the Great Gatsby's mansion or are enjoying passionate intercourse with the most beautiful woman on earth at a whim...?

This futuristic prophecy is not science fiction; it is readily available today. Just as the "Big Brother" concept introduced in George Orwell's masterpiece "1984", first published in 1944, is actually viable given today's technology. Just as the depiction of human dystopia in the 2008 animated film "WALL-E" as obese, largely immobile bodies of lard (while robots and machinery performed all duties & tasks), seem not so outlandish less than a decade later. Just as these two works illustrate, the same is true with the sensory manipulation capabilities described above.

Made in the USA
Las Vegas, NV
09 October 2023